THE CANADIAN IDENTITY

W.L. MORTON

The Canadian Identity

Second Edition

THE UNIVERSITY OF WISCONSIN PRESS

Published 1961, 1972
The University of Wisconsin Press
Box 1379, Madison, Wisconsin 53701
The University of Wisconsin Press, Ltd.
70 Great Russell Street, London

Second edition, 1972

Printed in United States of America
ISBN 0-299-06130-2 cloth, 0-299-06134-5 paper
LC 73-187505

Published in Canada by
University of Toronto Press
ISBN 0-8020-6139-7
Microfiche ISBN 0-8020-0186-6

A Note on the Second Edition

The four lectures published as *The Canadian Identity* in 1961 attracted more interest than expected, largely no doubt because their theme proved to be so timely. This measure of success seemed some reason to publish a second edition with a new chapter on the decade 1961–1971, a chapter already attempted in some historical detail to 1968 in the author's *The Kingdom of Canada* (2nd ed.).

In the present edition, the first four chapters have been left as they stood in 1961, except for two or three corrections already made in subsequent reprintings. The new chapter is a version, certainly contemporary, but perhaps not wholly unhistorical, of the main issues of the past decade in Canada. Faced with the problem of treating a single decade—and that, history's latest—in the same tone and on the same scale as some few centuries, of keeping the historian decently out of events, discussions, and emotions in which he had been involved, the writer has cast the new chapter in the past tense as though learned entirely from documents or eye-witnesses; he has even kept the mighty example of Thucydides, once the historian of his own country's failure, before his eyes, wryly and, it is hoped, with proper respect. For the inevitable distortions by lack of knowledge, unintentional prejudice, and faulty temper, the writer asks the reader's charity. For mistakes of fact and judgment he alone is responsible.

In the chapter added, nothing has been said directly of the Canadian identity, as indeed little was in the four lectures of the first edition. To the writer, the Canadian identity, the general and recognizable character of Canada, has always been clear enough. It is what their experience has made the Canadian people, a society made by history. Canada is a society growing by tradition, that "democracy of the dead." In a traditional society, society governs, and its members find themselves by serving that society. In that fact exists at once the weakness and the strength of Canada. Not for it the simple ethics of the joint-stock state, a limited agency for the collective realization of individual right, and the pursuit of profit as the chief end of man. But if in a traditional society becoming in fact ever more populist and pluralist, the tradition were not transmitted, the society would perish; only if it is transmitted from generation to generation can Canada survive.

Perhaps the basic discord of the past decade in Canada was that in both the great branches of the nation, the English and the French, men had passed under an a-historical mood. The English Canadian let his history slip, the French Canadian repudiated the last two centuries of his own. That they did so was in part because of their joint involvement in the general *malaise* of the decade, in part the failure of their historians to see Canada's history as a whole. But history is like nature; if expelled, it returns. It always reasserts itself.

Since the edition of 1961 appeared, the great gentleman and scholar, Paul Knaplund, under whose name and auspices the first three lectures were given, has passed to the Valhalla of scholars. The joyous vigour with which he lived strengthened all who knew him. As a student of the great liberal process by which Canada came into being, Knaplund too, it is fortifying to know, would have chastised the weakness of a decade in which Canada forgot the imperial origins from which it came, and he too would have taken for granted the survival of Canada as an independent nation in America.

I owe thanks to my University for time and means to complete this task; to my wife and friends who have borne my first and varied outbursts on the diverse themes of the new chapter; and to Miss Rita Young for weary work on the manuscript. My thanks are due also to the American audiences who listened to the first three chapters when delivered at the University of Wisconsin; should any of them read the new chapter, I trust that they will perceive that what is critical is meant for Canadians.

W.L.M.

Trent University
January 1, 1971

Preface to the First Edition

The four chapters which make up this book were first written and delivered as lectures: the first three as university lectures at the University of Wisconsin, while the author was Paul Knaplund Professor of Commonwealth History in the second semester of 1959–60, the fourth as a presidential address to the Canadian Historical Association at Queen's University in June, 1960. They appear as delivered, except for minor corrections and revisions, and the excision or condensation of repetitive material in the fourth lecture. The full text of that paper, of course, will appear in the Report of the Canadian Historical Association for 1960.

The lectures are an attempt to state, with such candor and point as the author could command, the character of Canadian nationhood in its peculiarly intimate association with the Commonwealth of Nations and the United States of America. In doing so, he was groping for some effective expression of Canadian identity, and publishes these chapters in the hope he has not entirely failed.

The statement is largely re-statement, of course, but it is made at a time of rapid evolution in the Commonwealth and of growing concern in Canada with the course and character of American-Canadian relations. Uncertainty as to the future of the Commonwealth and concern for the future of American-Canadian relations inform the pages which follow, and that there is some cause for both uncertainty and concern, few, it is supposed, would deny.

Nevertheless, the author, as a result of preparing this book, feels confident of two things. The first is that the future of the Commonwealth depends upon its success in maintaining in principle, and extending in practice, racial equality within as well as between its members. The recognition of racial equality is now fundamental to the existence of the Commonwealth. The second is that, serious as may be the causes for concern with American-Canadian relations, there is nothing in those causes which may not be put right by Canadian action, if Canadians are prepared to make the effort and to meet any cost that may be involved. If they are not so prepared, then they must expect to have to write off their separate history as a failure at once inglorious and insignificant.

With that certainty goes a likelihood amounting to certainty that, if Canadians should care to make themselves masters in their own household and act as they may think right and in Canada's interest in foreign policy, Americans will applaud—not all Americans, no doubt, but certainly those interested in Canada and not less those concerned with human freedom in all its variety and with genuine national character in the rising countries of the world.

They will applaud, however, only if they are convinced by Canadian performance that Canadian freedom is based on unshakable moral foundations and that Canadian nationhood is, in fact, a fruitful experiment of dignity and value.

The central point and statement of the book is, then, that if Canada is to continue to enjoy independence in association with the Commonwealth and the United States, it must achieve a self-definition of greater clarity and more ringing tone than it has yet done. It is to this task that Canadian statesmen must consciously address themselves in policy and by legislation. It is to this task, one hopes, that Canadian writers, historians, artists, and scientists, in the exacting pursuit of their own crafts and callings, may contribute indirectly, but decisively. It is finally a task to which every Canadian must bring whatever he has of heart and head. And all must be done in good humour and without animosity, as would befit perhaps the most fortunate country on earth and times in which all sovereignties are becoming conditional and all nations something less than independent.

It remains to express a gratitude, warm with the memory of many kindnesses and much helpful criticism, to my colleagues and students of the Departments of Geography and History of the University of Wisconsin; to acknowledge in particular my debt to Professor Paul Knaplund and Mrs. Knaplund for their interest in the lectures and their hospitality to Mrs. Morton and myself; and to thank my colleagues of the Council of the Canadian Historical Association for their permission to publish my presidential address as part of this book; also Major C. C. J. Bond for preparing the map, and Miss Dorothy Newman of the University of Manitoba for her help and patience in typing original drafts and final copy.

Responsibility for the faults and errors of the book remains as usual with their author.

W. L. M.

London, England
December 3, 1960

Contents

xi

THE CANADIAN IDENTITY

Chapter 1

Canada in America

The Character of Canadian Nationhood

Canada exists in America by the operation of geography, the needs of imperial strategy, the development of an historical tradition, and the conscious will of the Canadian people. It is not, more than other states, an historical accident or an artificial creation. It is an attempt to develop in a particular North American environment a civilization European in origin and American in evolution. Certain factors in its history and circumstances give a distinctive character to the development and existence of Canada. It is an attempt to maintain a modern nation-state, with an industrialized economy using a high technology, on a semicontinental scale, in a climate ranging from north temperate to arctic. It is an endeavour to allow two cultures to flourish in one political nationality. It is, finally, an effort to preserve a slowly evolved independence as the intimate neighbour of a great world power under the stress and novelty of the power politics of the nuclear age.

The Maritime Frontier and the Northern Economy

Canadian history began when the Vikings carried their maritime frontier of fish, fur, and farm across the North Atlantic to Iceland and Greenland. At the end of the fifteenth century that northern passage was resumed by the traders of Bristol and the fishermen of Normandy. From that obscure beginning Canada had a distinct, a unique, a northern destiny. Its modern beginnings are not Columbian but Cabotan. And when the French followed Cartier up the St. Lawrence, they were at once committed by the development of the fur trade to the exploitation of the Canadian Shield. Their fishermen and fur traders, even their *habitants,* established the maritime and northern frontier of the North Atlantic along the great river of Canada and the Shield, which overlooks from its blue escarpment the distant river in its valley lands.

The Canadian, or Precambrian, Shield is as central in Canadian history as it is to Canadian geography, and to all understanding of Canada. It is almost one half of all Canadian territory[1] and sweeps in a vast crescent from the Strait of Belle Isle by the St. Lawrence and the Lakes to the Canadian lakes of the Northwest and the mouth of the Mackenzie. It holds like a saucer the great inland sea of Hudson Bay. It throws up in Labrador and Baffin Island mountains that almost challenge the Rockies which balance it on the Pacific, and along its southern rim heaves up its granite and glacier-scored shoulders in geologic defiance of four Ice Ages survived and of those yet to come. So strong that not even the contraction of the globe itself has buckled its rigidity, it remains with its naked granite ridges, its multitudinous waters and sodden muskegs, an enduring contrast to the wide and fertile lands, the gentle slopes and hardwood forests of the Mississippi valley. The heartland of the United States is one of earth's most fertile regions, that of Canada one of earth's most ancient wildernesses and one of nature's grimmest challenges to man and all his works. No Canadian has found it necessary

1. Some 1,800,000 of 3,800,000 square miles.

seriously to revise Cartier's spontaneous comment as he gazed on the Labrador coast of the Shield. It was, he said in awe, "the land that God gave Cain." The main task of Canadian life has been to make something of this formidable heritage.

There has, in fact, always been something to be made of the Shield, provided a base was available on which to grow food and on which to prepare for the penetration and exploitation of the Shield. In Canadian history the St. Lawrence valley, the Ontario peninsula, and the western prairies have been the regions of settlement which have furnished and fed the men, the fur traders, the lumberjacks, the prospectors, and the miners who have traversed the Shield and wrested from it the staples by which Canada has lived. And this alternate penetration of the wilderness and return to civilization is the basic rhythm of Canadian life, and forms the basic elements of Canadian character whether French or English, the violence necessary to contend with the wilderness, the restraint necessary to preserve civilization from the wilderness violence, and the puritanism which is the offspring of the wedding of violence to restraint. Even in an industrial and urban society, the old rhythm continues, for the typical Canadian holiday is a wilderness holiday, whether among the lakes of the Shield or the peaks of the Rockies.

The quest for furs carried the Canadians of the seventeenth century along the southern edge of the Shield into the interior of the continent. The missionaries and *coureurs de bois* of New France overran the interior of the continent in the third quarter of the century. So great a distance inland set them searching for easier outlets than the long voyage back by the Ottawa and the St. Lawrence. Groseilliers and Radisson turned to Hudson Bay for such an outlet, La Salle to the Mississippi. By 1697 one of the greatest of Canadians, Pierre le Moyne d'Iberville, had conquered all but one English post on Hudson Bay and all but two English outposts on Newfoundland. Then he turned to the mouth of the Mississippi where he began the founding of Louisiana. Had the French negotiators not restored the Newfoundland fish-

THE ST. LAWRENCE
FRONTIER IN 1755

Quebec
Ste. Foy
Trois
Rivières
CANADA
Montreal
Ottawa R.
ST. LAWRENCE R.
Richelieu R.
(45° LAT)
Lake
Champlain
Fort Frontenac
(KINGSTON)
Toronto
LAKE
ONTARIO
Ft. St. Frédéric
(CROWN POINT)
Carillon
(TICONDEROGA)
Lake George
Ft. William Henry
Oswego
YORK
NEW
Mohawk R.
Hudson R.
50   0   50   100
MILES

ATLANTIC

OCEAN

GREENLAND

ETH

FRANKLIN BAFFIN
ISLAND

ERRITORIES

HUDSON

of Wales
(churchill)

A
BAY

TORNGAT
MTNS

A

N E W F O U N D

COAST OF
GOOSE
LABRADOR   Bay

QUEBEC

SHIELD

EASTERN
TOWNSHIPS

NTARIO

inistiquia
WILLIAM)

Sudbury

Quebec

Montreal

OTTAWA

U. S.
BASES

St. John's

ST. PIERRE &
MIQUELON
(FRANCE)

FISHING   BANKS

GULF
OF
ST. LAWRENCE

CAPE
Louisbourg
BRETON I.

PRINCE
EDWARD

NEW
BRUNSWICK

NOVA SCOTIA

Halifax

ACADIA DURING
THE FRENCH
REGIME

Saint
John

Fort Beauséjour
St. John River
St. Croix River

Ft.
Michilimackinac
(FRENCH)

airie
du
hien

Detroit

ONTARIO
PENINSULA

Toronto
Niagara

Hudson R.

Ft. Le Boeuf

THE ATLANTIC
PROVINCES
OVERLAP

Ft. Duquesne (PITTSBURGH)

Ohio R.

opi
R.

THE ONTARIO
PENINSULA
OVERLAP

THE EASTERN
TOWNSHIPS
OVERLAP

ery to England, this Canadian soldier of the fur trade and member of *la grande bourgeoisie canadienne* would have briefly held for Canada and himself three of the four entries to North America.

The French Bid for Empire in America, 1700–1760

All this endeavour was largely private and much of it was carried on in defiance of the wishes and policy of the French court. Then by one of those sudden external changes which have so often altered the destiny of Canada, French imperial policy suddenly came into line with the aspirations and interests of Canada. Louis XIV accepted the Spanish succession on behalf of his grandson, and at once it became desirable to interpose a French barrier between the Spanish possessions in America and the English colonies on the Atlantic seaboard. Then Iberville's Louisiana, little more at first than an outlet for Canadian *coureurs de bois* who had reason not to go home to Montreal, became part of a Bourbon imperial design. France was to bid for supremacy in America, and the Canadian penetration of the interior was a card already played. While, however, Canada was to see its most ardent hopes realized, it was at the same time as a mere fur trade colony of 12,000 people now part, for good or ill, of the European balance of power finally and fully extended to America.

The decision of Louis to accept the reversion of the Spanish Empire for the House of Bourbon precipitated the War of the Spanish Succession. That was, however, a European war which led to little fighting in America. Only in Acadia and Newfoundland did the guerrilla warfare of the previous conflict flare up. Elsewhere a practical, almost a formal, truce prevailed until 1709. Then the rise of the Tories to power in England, with the change of the character of the English war effort from a European to a colonial war, and the strengthening of the French hold on the fur trade of the west, led to the outbreak of hostilities. But the only outcome was the capture of Acadia; the Walker-Hill expedition against Quebec failed before the hazards of the navigation of the St. Lawrence.

The outcome of the peace negotiations, however, was entirely different. All Hudson Bay was ceded; all Newfoundland but the "French shore"; all Acadia "within its ancient limits" except Cape Breton Island. Moreover, the British claim to suzerainty over the Five Nations was recognized, as was the right of the English to trade with the western tribes. In effect, the French bid for empire in America was defeated; supremacy passed by the Treaty of Utrecht to the Anglo-Americans. The persistent resistance of the French negotiators had saved the Newfoundland fishery and the entry to the Gulf of St. Lawrence. But New France was left with only the slender exit by the St. Lawrence; its vital fur trade was riddled from south and north by the traders of New York and of the Hudson's Bay Company. Louisiana was untouched, but its tribes too were under the growing influence of the fur trade of the southern Anglo-American colonies. The empire of New France might almost be said to have survived on sufferance, were it not that its rivals could not yet achieve the co-ordination and technical proficiency necessary for the decisive campaign against the Laurentian stronghold of Quebec.

Time was left New France, then, to recover and recoup. The fur trade was restored; the western posts, centring on Michilimackinac, were slowly strengthened; the trade spread west and north despite the savage opposition of the Foxes in the two wars of extermination fought on the soil of Wisconsin between the Canadians and that obdurate tribe from 1714 to 1738. And even before the Foxes were subdued, Canadian troops had to go to the help of Louisiana in the Chickasaw war. These commercial wars with the English-supported tribes tried the strength of New France severely, but peace had been established in the interior by 1738. On the Atlantic coast the building of the great fortress of Louisbourg on Cape Breton Island began in 1720, to harbour the fleet that was to guard the Gulf and overawe the New Englanders. The building of Oswego on Lake Ontario by the New Yorkers in 1726 was a heavy setback, but it was countered by fortifying the post at Niagara in 1727. In 1731 Fort Saint Frédéric was built on Lake Champlain to stop the route of invasion from New York, that fur-trading, feudal colony, so like New France and so much its most deadly enemy.

Then, in the same year, Pierre Gaultier, sieur de la Vérendrye of Trois Rivières, once left for dead on the field of Malplaquet, began his advance from Kaministiquia on Lake Superior to the basin of Red River. By 1744 his posts stood ranged from Rainy Lake to the lower Saskatchewan, and furs which had once gone down to York Factory now went to Montreal. As was to happen once again in Canadian history, the Northwest had been called in to restore the balance of the continent.

The extent of New France in 1744 was more imposing than ever; its strength had been largely restored. It was, however, a brittle and unstable structure. Canada and Louisiana were rivals, at odds over the Illinois country and competing for the fur trade. Had Hudson Bay been French, its trade would still have been competitive with that of Canada. Canada itself, the *seigneurial* lands with their three towns of fortress Quebec, fur-trading Trois Rivières, and clerical-commercial Montreal, the Canada of the river-front villages ranged along the St. Lawrence and the Richelieu, was as peaceful and civilized as any New England township or Virginia plantation. The oxen plodded in the furrow; the church bells called along the rivers; the robed fathers and white-cowled nuns moved through the narrow streets on their ministrations of mercy. But the French empire in America was a barbarous alliance of Canadian fur trader and Indian, an alliance already cemented by their mixed blood progeny of the *métis*. Such an alliance could hold the vast interior only for the fur trade; it could hold only by that mixture of commerce, diplomacy, and war which was the fur trade; it could hold only against numbers and warfare similar to its own. Only the military power and diplomacy of Old France, that is, could maintain the empire of the

New in America, should England and its colonies organize their
resources in America.

The essential weakness of New France was revealed by the
War of the Austrian Succession. The long Anglo-French *entente*
of Walpole and Fleury which had given New France its time for
recovery had broken down by 1742. In 1744 England joined in
the continental war against France. Again, England chose to
fight a continental war and to leave America in peace. But the
New Englanders, long irritated by Louisbourg, took it in a brilliant campaign with the aid of an English squadron and opened
the way to Quebec in 1745. A campaign against Canada was
planned in England, but in the year after Fontenoy and when the
Highlands of Scotland were at last being conquered, it was not
surprising that the expedition was not readied in time for depar-
ture. France did try to recover Louisbourg, but the first expedition was scattered by storm, and perished miserably of disease in
what was shortly to be Halifax harbour, the second was caught by
an English squadron off Cape Finisterre. The New Englanders
held Louisbourg until they were reminded that they were subjects of a world-wide empire, in which fortresses were sometimes
lost as well as won, by the British diplomats exchanging it for
Madras in distant India.

The war thus ended inconclusively. But a number of things
had happened in its course which were to have decisive consequences. The first was that France failed to hold at the peace the
advantages it had won in Europe. A second was that the difficulties of communication with France had reduced the supply of
French trade goods and raised the prices of what there were. As
a result the western tribes were drawn from the French posts to
settle in the long-vacant lands on the upper Ohio where they
could trade for English goods with the Iroquois and the Anglo-
American traders, who now began to come over the mountains in
numbers to trade. Suddenly this country, long masked by the Iroquois power, came into Canadian history.

Another event of the war of no less consequence than the above was the dispatch of a man of first-rate mind to govern New France. This was the Marquis de la Galissonnière.[2] A commander of high talent and great strategic flair, a *philosophe* and a polished courtier, La Galissonnière for the first time brought to Canadian affairs the outlook and purposes of European power politics. He had wished to fight the late war in America with vigour. Denied that by the peace, he had written to Versailles to insist that France must hold America in order to deny it to the Anglo-Americans. To hold it, it must hold not only Canada, but the line of the Ohio. Acting at once, he sent Céleron de Blainville to claim the Ohio. He himself then returned to France, but his successors carried out his policy. In 1753, 2,200 *troupes de la marine* and Canadian militia toiled in the fierce Ohio heat to fortify the portage from Lake Erie to the headwaters of *la belle rivière*. It was an effort from which Canada had not recovered when the war it provoked broke out. Then at the Fort le Boeuf he had just finished, the Canadian commander, Jacques Repentigny Legardeur de Saint-Pierre, fresh down from the commanding in the Northwest, received a sober young gentleman from Virginia who advised him he was trepassing on the lands of His Britannic Majesty. Saint-Pierre replied politely but firmly to George Washington that on the contrary they were the lands of His Most Christian Majesty and that he had orders to remain where he had been posted. The issue of which power, France or England, was to dominate America and endow it with its institutions, was fully drawn as the fur trader from the Assiniboine faced the planter from Virginia on the headwaters of the Ohio.

Washington's subsequent expedition of 1754 and his surrender at Fort Necessity left the Canadians in possession of the Ohio. Fort Duquesne was built at the Forks and the Canadian claim to the valley was made good. It was held against Braddock in 1755

2. The role of La Galissonnière in Canadian history requires a fuller treatment than it has yet received. He was actually sent, not as Governor General, but as lieutenant for the Marquis de la Jonquière, who had been captured in the naval action off Finisterre in 1747.

and the preparations for the great trial of strength in America went forward. As the British sent Braddock and regular troops to contest the Ohio, so the French sent Baron Dieskau with *regiments de terre*. The white and the blue-coated regulars of France were to form points of strength around which the Canadian militia and the Indian allies, mission Indians from the St. Lawrence and Ottawas from the upper Lakes, were to wage a defensive campaign of *la petite guerre* in the old Canadian tradition. The French professionals and the Canadian irregulars combined even less happily than the British line and the American militia. The French commanders bickered with the Canadian-born governor and commander-in-chief, Vaudreuil; the French regulars looked with suspicion and dismay on their undisciplined and barbarous allies.

None the less, the French might have held the few passes of the long forest frontier from the Ohio to the Richelieu, had the rise of Pitt not given a decisive turn to the character of the war. It is true that Fort Beauséjour at Chignecto was lost in 1755 and the Acadians deported; it is true that William Johnson defeated and captured Dieskau at Fort William Henry on Lake George in 1756. Yet the French held the Hudson-Richelieu line and took Oswego and Loudoun failed to move against Louisbourg in 1757. But in that year Pitt assumed direction of the war. Behind him were the great merchant houses of London, demanding the expansion of British trade in America and India. Behind him were the governors and people of New England and New York, demanding an end of the French and Indian menace on their borders. His own genius, vain, arrogant, and not a little mad, drove him on. It would be, he decided, a war of maritime and colonial conquest. Britain would hold in Germany and strike in America. It would strike for absolute victory and supremacy in America. Pitt was the counter to La Galissonnière. Cut off, over-strained, exhausted New France sent Bougainville to Versailles in the fall of 1758 to plead for help. Little could be offered and he returned with orders to hold to the end.

The build-up and the attack followed. Canada had won the greatest of its victories at Carillon in 1758, but Amherst had taken Louisbourg and opened the sea gates of Canada. Forbes had cut his way to Duquesne and renamed it Fort Pitt. In 1759 Amherst, ever deliberate, opened the way on Lake Champlain to Montreal, but failed to push on. The thrusting Bradstreet somewhat redeemed the western campaign when he took Oswego and Frontenac. There could then be no fighting retreat to the Mississippi. Wolfe surprised Montcalm into the hasty and fated battle on the heights at Quebec, but failed to capture the French army. It escaped and lived to fight another year, gathering the laurels of Sainte Foy in the spring of 1760. But then the three poised Anglo-American armies closed in on Montreal. The Anglo-Americans had organized their numbers, isolated their objectives and won.

French empire in America ended with the Treaty of Paris. Only the French shore in Newfoundland and the islands of Saint Pierre and Miquelon were left, to nourish the French fishery and French naval power. But the French colony in Canada, not yet to be called a nation, survived as a French and a Catholic community. Behind it was the wild up-country of the fur trade. Its posts were garrisoned now, it is true, by British, not French, troops, but they were also British, not American, troops. From these two facts was to come the survival of Canada, a Canada that in its deepest psyche was never to forget the bid for supremacy and the loss of empire in America.

The Disruption of the Anglo-American Empire, 1763–1783

The Anglo-American conquest of Canada marked the end of colonial and the beginning of imperial British America. Indeed, the dispatches of La Galissonnière and the founding of Halifax, with their initiation of direct intervention in America by the imperial power of France and the United Kingdom, had marked the beginning of the end of the old colonial order, characterized in both New France and the English colonies by great latitude for commercial enterprise and local self-government and by a surprisingly small measure of imperial regulation.

The new imperial order, however, was still incipient only. There had not yet emerged the concepts, the institutions, or the leaders to create the general government which would give coherence and direction to the new empire in America and ensure that the existing liberty of the colonists would be reconciled with the authority necessary for empire. In the Albany Congress of 1754, which met in the most imperial of the English colonies on the border of the great interior wilderness of the Indian and the fur trade, the men assembled had a clear vision of what was required if America was to be united under one government. But both the colonists and the Imperial authorities drew back in fear of the power which such a government might develop. It would be too much to say that an opportunity was lost; a scheme so premature was not an opportunity but only a premonition. Not for thirty-five years could Americans bring themselves to submit to a general government with real authority.

There was, however, no drawing back from the path of continental empire in the peace negotiations which ended the Seven Years' War. In the famous debate as to whether Canada or Guadeloupe should be retained, the Canadian wilderness prevailed over the tropical sugar island. Canada was not kept for its wealth. It was held in order that it and its wild hinterlands might be suppressed within the Anglo-American empire and that empire made safe from the border warfare and continental encirclement for which Canada had stood. The Anglo-American empire, a dominion from the unknown arctic coast to the Gulf of Mexico and from the coast of Labrador to the left bank of the Mississippi, was reared on the defeat and obliteration of Canada. The map of New France was wiped clean.

On the new map the Royal Proclamation of October, 1763, laid down a province of Quebec. Its borders confined it to the valley of the lower St. Lawrence, and almost to those lands granted by the Crown of France as *seigneuries*. The western boundary cut across the St. Lawrence not far above Montreal. Quebec was New France shorn of its western and northern hinterlands and cut down to the original Canada of the lower St. Lawrence.

The Proclamation, moreover, and the instructions to the new civil governor, General James Murray, provided and assumed that it would be a royal colony of the conventional type, governed by governor and council and given local laws by an assembly. As only Protestants could vote or hold office under English law, these provisions obviously assumed that the creation of the new province would be followed by an influx of British and Protestant settlers. The temporary closing by the Proclamation of the lands west of the Alleghenies to settlement made it clear that such was the intent of the Imperial government.

The actual government of Quebec in the years immediately following 1764 wholly thwarted the Imperial policy. Governor Murray declined to summon an assembly because such a body would have been made up only of the representatives of some five hundred "old subjects," who would then have had power to make laws affecting the lives and property of the some seventy thousand "new subjects." Yet without an assembly no new laws could be made and no taxes levied. In this deadlock the government of Quebec was held for ten years.

The control of the hinterlands of New France had in effect been assumed by the Imperial government itself when it issued the Proclamation of 1763. The Empire had absorbed the French and Indian frontier and had now to police it. By so doing, it assumed the task of maintaining peace with the Indian tribes of the Ohio country and the Southwest, and of obtaining the title to sufficient Indian land to allow the migration of Anglo-American settlers across the mountains to proceed without recurrent Indian wars. At the same time the Imperial government faced the task of disentangling the conflicting colonial claims under the charters to the transmontane lands. It thus entered one of the most contentious areas of colonial politics. Even more daunting was the prospect of having to erect colonial governments hundreds of miles inland. Hitherto the British Empire, mercantile and maritime as it was, had nowhere, not even in India, a dependency which could not be reached by sea. To those who thought about it, the prospect of a great territorial empire was unpleasant and even unnerving.

The situation, moreover, called for speedy and resolute action. The American colonists were eager to reap the fruits of the absolute victory in the French and Indian War. The settlers were already moving across the mountains. New Indian wars and ungovernable settlements were already imminent. The northern superintendent of Indian affairs, Sir William Johnson, strove to persuade the sullen and suspicious tribes to negotiate and to surrender some of their lands. Little was accomplished by the Treaty of Fort Stanwix in 1768. The failure is in part to be explained by the lack of stable administrations in the United Kingdom between 1763 and 1770, but even more was it the consequence of the want of an Imperial apparatus in America through which the Imperial government and the American colonists might together and on the spot have provided a government for the western lands which might perhaps have dealt with the conflicting claims of colonies, land speculators, settlers, Indians, and fur traders.

There was no such apparatus. In default of a general government in America, the Imperial government proceeded to deal individually and directly with the issues arising out of the incorporation of New France in the Anglo-American empire. The deadlock in Quebec came first to their attention. The "old subjects" had procured the recall of Murray in 1766. But the advent of his successor, Guy Carleton, did not mean their triumph and that of the policy of the Proclamation. After some delay, Carleton adopted Murray's stand that the policy of 1763 would work an intolerable injustice on the French-Canadians. In fact, the policy of 1763 might have been made just and tolerable by admitting Roman Catholics to public office in the province, as the Board of Trade was to recommend in 1770. But Carleton had other objects in view. French power was reviving in Europe, particularly that of the French navy; the ships were building that in 1781 were to stand between Cornwallis and evacuation from Yorktown. There was trouble in the colonies to the south. The Indians of the west were a constant preoccupation. In the face of all these possible dangers, one thing stood out. Quebec was the garrison colony of the Anglo-American empire. About half the regular troops in America were in Quebec and the western posts until 1770. If that garrison were to hold America against French attack, Indian war, or colonial rebellion, it could not be used to put down a Canadian guerrilla. Justice to the Canadians had therefore a strategic purpose. It would conciliate them, and, Carleton hoped, bind them to the British cause. For the Irish soldier, like Murray, had responded to the natural courtesy and the military spirit of the Canadians of the old regime and hoped to win their loyalty by reopening to them the military and official careers lost by the cession.

To ensure that his views should prevail, Carleton went to England in 1770 and remained there until 1774. That year saw the passage of the Quebec Act. The Act was the outcome of the want of a general government for the British North American empire. Since there was no general American government to control the old French and Indian empire, and since local self-government for the French province seemed to be too great to risk in the circumstances, a new kind of local and Imperial government was invented for Quebec. It was made a Crown colony by Act of Parliament. Roman Catholics were admitted to public office, but there was to be no representative legislature, at least for the time being, and Parliament by a second Act provided customs duties to raise a revenue. The concessions to Roman Catholics and the Roman Catholic Church, together with the constitution and taxation provided by the Imperial parliament, made the Quebec Act offensive and menacing to the Anglo-American colonists. The last minute addition to the government of Quebec, subject to the rights of the old colonies, of the lands between the Ohio

and the Mississippi, of course added to their fear and anger. Coupled as it was in their minds with the Coercive Acts, it was impossible for the colonists to see the Quebec Act for what it was, an attempt to do justice to the Canadians and to provide a further temporary government for the Northwest Indian frontier. To them, the Imperial parliament had revived the French and Indian menace to coerce them, and had disrupted the empire of 1763.

The American reaction was instant and illuminating. Before the war for independence had begun, they fought a prior war, that of 1775–76.[3] It was a war for the unity of the Anglo-American empire. It was a war that had to be fought, as the Quebec Act had to be passed, because of the lack of some Imperial apparatus to govern and control the French and Indian frontier incorporated in that empire by the Treaty of Paris. It was also a war fought between the British and the Americans. Some Canadians joined the Americans; some fought for the British; the great majority, unmoved by either Parliament or Congress, remained neutral. The issue of Imperial unity seemed to them, before they had time to digest the implications of the Quebec Act, to have nothing to do with their own desire to survive as a French and Catholic community.

Thus the decisive element in the war for American unity was the intervention of British naval and military power in the spring of 1776. The American troops had to abandon the seige of Quebec and vacate Canada. Canada remained a British garrison and military base, as Nova Scotia also did. That was the immediate result; the long-range result, as the seven years' War of Independence was to reveal, was that Canada had been liberated from the Anglo-American empire. The French and Indian border and the northern economy of the fur trade had risen from the grave of 1763.

There was no more fighting on Canadian soil after 1776, except

3. This fact, usually overlooked, is pointed out by S. D. Clark in his *Movements of Political Protest in Canada, 1640–1840* (Toronto, 1959), p. 50.

George Rogers Clark's raid on the Illinois country in 1778. Except for two major operations, Canada lay in the background of the War of Independence which was fought for the control of the seaboard rather than of the interior. One of those operations was the prolonged civil war of patriot and loyalist in which the New York frontier tore itself apart. New York, the colony most like Canada, was also the most loyalist. There American fought American more bitterly than elsewhere; there the British and the loyalists held out to the end. The feudal loyalty of the Johnsons and the Butlers, the ties of the fur trade, the old alliance of the Iroquois, all served to keep many upstate New Yorkers loyal to the Crown. Harried from their mansions and their farmsteads, they made Canada their base on the St. Lawrence and the Niagara, and struck back in raids recalling those of the Hertels and the Vaudreuils. American legend long exaggerated the savagery of this warfare, but it was the old warfare of the French and Indian frontier revived and intensified. It hampered Washington, it helped to save Canada from reconquest, and its memory lay long between the people it divided.

The other operation was Burgoyne's attack along the Richelieu-Hudson line. Canada was at last to see struck the blow which Frontenac had once planned. A campaign by the Richelieu-Hudson line was the classic stroke of the old colonial warfare. Burgoyne's rendering of it, like Amherst's and Montgomery's, was meant to be decisive. Unlike theirs, it was, but by its catastrophe, not its triumph. The surrender at Saratoga ensured American independence. It is seldom noted that, for similar reasons, it ensured Canadian independence also. The same French allies who helped America to independence also imposed a check on victorious America's again attempting the conquest of Canada.

Canada, the Canada of the St. Lawrence, it was probable by 1779, was not to be part of the new American empire. But what of the hinterland between the Ohio and the Mississippi? Here too, the cause of the Canadian alliance of Indian and fur trader,

of wilderness and distance, was to prevail. The border raids of
la petite guerre had perhaps their greatest day between 1779
and 1781 on the Niagara and Ohio frontiers. Sullivan's campaign
of 1779 in western New York checked the loyalists on the Niagara frontier; the death of Walter Butler at West Canada Creek in
1782 marked the end of the raiding into New York. But no American army saw the vital line of the St. Lawrence and the Lakes.
No American Forbes marched to the Ohio. The settlements Clark
had taken were recaptured. In 1780 a Canadian party from Michilimackinac even struck at the Spaniards in St. Louis.[4] Canada had held the line of the Ohio and the vast interior.

The Second Loss of Continental Empire, 1783

Canada had won its war, but it was to have no hand in the
peace. The War of Independence had become one of the great
world wars of the eighteenth century. The conflict ranged from
the west coast of Hudson Bay, where La Pérouse destroyed Prince
of Wales Fort, to the Coromandel coast of India where Admirals
Hughes and Suffren hammered one another in eight drawn en-
gagements. In the struggle Britain had stood alone against the
House of Bourbon and the armed neutrality of Northern Europe.
No ally had fought its battles in Germany. When Yorktown made
the recognition of the American independence inevitable, the aim
of British diplomacy was simply to make a peace as little disas-
trous as possible by seeking to divide its enemies. Since the
Americans had to be conceded independence anyway, clearly the
concession must be made in such a way as to separate them from
their coalition with the European imperial powers. The peace
with America must therefore be a peace of conciliation.

---

4. These forgotten campaigns may be followed in H. Swiggett's *War Out
of Niagara* (New York, 1933) and John D. Barnhart, *Henry Hamilton and
George Rogers Clark in the American Revolution* (Crawfordsville, Ind.,
1951). It is characteristic of the two countries that they are embodied in
American legend and literature, and as such widely known in Canada,
while the loyalist legends are practically forgotten and the fighting and the
men who fought ignored, even in Canadian historical literature.

What the Americans wanted was independence and the unity of the British America of 1763, together with a resumption of trade and re-entry into the northeastern fisheries. Three of these four aims might have been conceded by the cession of Canada, Nova Scotia, Newfoundland, and the Hudson Bay territory. Franklin in the opening, informal talks suggested this obvious truth, adding that it would ensure peace between Britain and her former colonies. The proposal was not thought audacious and was reported by the British representative. But the protests of George III, the need to preserve a refuge for the loyalists and to maintain in Quebec and Halifax a strategic check on the new republic, combined to block so simple a solution. There was still to be a British America; the continent was to be divided. But how?

Why not, inquired Franklin's associate, John Jay of New York, simply extend the forty-fifth parallel, made the southern boundary of Quebec in 1763, indefinitely westward? Again the simple proposal had tremendous implications. Canada would survive, and with it the Northwest fur trade and the northern economy. British seapower would continue to hold Halifax and Quebec, and there would be a refuge for the loyalists. But the lands between the Ohio and the Mississippi, with the western posts except Michilimackinac, all held in eight years of fighting, would pass to the Americans. The interior empire of New France and British America would be surrendered to the United States.

The couriers and the dispatches crossed and recrossed the Channel. Finally, it was decided that the boundary would follow either the forty-fifth parallel or the line of the St. Lawrence and the Lakes. The British cabinet chose the latter. Then it was agreed that the boundary between Maine and Nova Scotia would begin at the St. Croix, and that from Lake Superior the northwest boundary would follow the fur traders' canoe route to the northwest angle of the Lake of the Woods and from there run west to the head of the Mississippi. The old empire of New France, with Nova Scotia, Newfoundland, and Hudson Bay, had

been held, but the country of the Lakes had been divided and the great triangle between the Ohio and the Mississippi, the heartland of North America, had been surrendered. For a second time Canada had lost this land which, if populated, spelled continental supremacy in America. It was confined to the Gulf and valley of the St. Lawrence and to the fur trade of the Shield and the far Northwest. Canada, it was obvious, was to be the country of the northern economy, the extension of the northern maritime frontier across the arctic slope of America.

The Confirmation of Continental Division, 1784–1814

The news of the boundary of 1783 produced consternation in Quebec and Montreal. Both the soldiers and the traders saw that Britain in 1783, like France in 1763, had abandoned its Indian allies. Both expected an Indian rising, the plundering of the posts, and perhaps a resumption of the war in the west. They persuaded the Imperial government to keep the garrisons in the posts from Oswego to Michilimackinac, and to continue to give the Indians the presents and supplies which were the staples of Indian diplomacy. An excuse for this violation of the treaty was found in the refusal of the American states to make restitution to the loyalists or to allow pre-war British creditors access to the courts. The result was of course that much of the land south of the Lakes continued to be disputed with the Americans by the tribes which felt that in the last resort the British would support them.

There were those in British America who cherished similar hopes. Not only did the fur traders of Montreal hope to continue to hold the trade of the Southwest. Many leading loyalists hoped that the division of 1783 might be undone and the British empire in America reunited.

The two most obvious things about the loyalist refugees are often overlooked. One is that they were Americans, unreconstructed Americans. In the bitterness of exile their Americanism only intensified. The second is that, as their designation of United Empire Loyalist signified, they had fought for a united empire, an empire united in America as well as across the Atlantic. The ideal of a united empire in America they had given up no more than that of an empire united as between the mother country and the colonies. To them the defeat of 1781 was as incredible and as intolerable as the cession of the country of the Lakes was to the soldiers and traders of Canada. To undo it, to reverse somehow the decision of 1783, remained their hope down to 1814. British America, truncated as it was, was in the hearts of the loyalists a base around which the continental empire of 1763 might be reconstituted.

In a measure the reorganization of British America was coloured by the hopes of the loyalist leaders. To most British statesmen the loss of the American colonies had been a wounding experience. A nation which prided itself on its ancient and well established freedom could not readily believe that it had lessons in liberty to learn from its offspring in America. They tended therefore to look for the causes of American independence, not in American devotion to liberty, which liberty they felt had never been threatened, but in defects of the old colonial institutions. These defects, they decided, had been a lamentable weakness in the executive government of the colonies and an even more lamentable excess of democracy in the colonial constitutions. The American governments, they affirmed, and any American conservative of the day would have understood them perfectly, had not known a just division of powers and a proper balance of the monarchical, aristocratic, and democratic elements. These faults they proceeded to correct in the remaining continental colonies by insuring that the governors had a revenue independent of the assemblies, and that the Legislative Councils actually served as second chambers and buffers between the governor and the democratic assembly. Thus the assemblies, while in no wise deprived of their representative character, were checked and balanced by independent executives and upper chambers. Finally, in some slight acknowledgement of the wisdom of the Albany

Americans directly affected, with the exception of impressed American seamen, were not themselves injured and were sympathetic with Britain in her war against revolutionary France. In the Napoleonic War after 1803 the Republican administrations got more popular support in their efforts to stop the British infringements, especially after the attack on the U.S.S. *Chesapeake* in 1807. But the American government had no thought of going to war about the issues, important as they were, until in 1812 Macon's Bill No. 2 and Napoleon's sharp manoeuvre in rescinding the Berlin decrees forced Madison to declare war, or make the United States ridiculous before the world.

Thus "Mr. Madison's war" was an inadvertent one and, it proved, quite unnecessary, as the British also had withdrawn the offensive Orders in Council. Moreover, the war was highly unpopular, especially in New England. It had, however, to be fought, and must therefore be made popular if possible. The west was the place to win comparatively cheap and easy victories. An Indian war was already in progress in the American Southwest and in the Northwest the alliance formed by Tecumseh and the Prophet had been defeated at Tippecanoe in 1811. Behind the northwestern tribes were the Canadian traders and the British garrisons. A war against Canada would finally break the Indians, and might be used to "liberate" the Canadians. Thus a war rightly declared to assert maritime rights was inexorably transformed into the last of the old border wars for continental supremacy.

If the American government and generals needed a quick and showy victory, so did their enemies. Since the crisis of 1807 Canada had been readied for war. The British regular battalions were in good trim; something had been made of the Canadian militia by the conciliating tact of Sir George Prevost in Lower Canada and the military zeal and soldierly charm of Sir Isaac Brock in Upper Canada. Moreover, since New England refused to fight and eastern New York was almost equally unwilling, Lower Canada had a protective buffer in what was in effect neutral territory. The strategic problem was therefore how to ensure that the American settlers in Upper Canada stayed at home, and how to win the Indians to recapture the lost territory of the upper Lakes. The answer was a quick victory to bring the Indians, still shaken by Tippecanoe, into the war on the British side. Canada would once more fight a French and Indian war.

The Canadian fur trade had always fought almost as readily as it traded. As with the Indians, war and trade went hand in hand; war was trade conducted by other means. In mid-July, 1812, a few British regulars with some hundreds of Canadians and Indians captured Michilimackinac. The victory had far-reaching consequences; all the country west of the Lakes fell to the British, and by 1814 they were once more on the Mississippi at Prairie du Chien. More important was the fact that the Michigan peninsula fell to them, and General William Hull at Detroit, knowing the Indians were swarming on his line of communications, surrendered to Brock in early August.

Such was the initial character of the war. Its course cannot be traced here. It must suffice to say that in Canada it ended with the Americans holding the western portion of the Upper Canada peninsula from recaptured Detroit, and the British holding the country of the upper Lakes and Maine. But Prevost had been stopped on the Richelieu-Hudson line, and Pakenham was stopped at New Orleans. If the Americans had failed to conquer Canada, the British had failed to lever the republic apart. Federalist dissension and the Hartford Convention, the smoke that revealed there were some sparks to warm the ancient loyalist hopes, perhaps came nearer to threatening the union of the states than did the Peninsular veterans of Wellington. Certain it is that with the Hartford Convention and the impeachment of Chief Justice Sewell of Lower Canada for, among other things, attempting to bring New England into the Empire, ended the last lingering hopes of the loyalists.[5] It therefore seemed better to end an unintended war which had so startlingly awakened the old continental ambitions and set the war parties raiding and the armies

5. See W. H. Nelson, "The Last Hopes of the American Loyalists," *Canadian Historical Review*, Mar., 1956, pp. 22–43.

marching again along the old familiar war routes. The peace put the boundaries where they had been before. The peace settlement came later.

The Final Division of the Continent, 1818–1846

The men who made the peace settlement of 1817–18 in the aftermath of the treaties of Ghent and Vienna were men of large vision and much restraint. They had seen a world broken and reconstituted. They knew the elements of power, the weakness and uncertainty that made for war, the balance of forces which made for peace and could by time be transmuted into right. The War of 1812 had made it clear that the defence of Upper Canada, or its conquest, depended on naval control of the Lakes. To prevent a resumption of the naval race the war had started, the Lakes were disarmed except for police vessels by the Rush-Bagot convention of 1817. This seemingly simple act registered the fact that if British sea power could blockade the Atlantic coast at will, American land power could cross the Canadian border when it would. The convention registered that balance of power, on which the relations of British America and the United States rested for the remainder of the century. Then a convention of 1818, besides once more trying to settle the northeastern boundary, laid down the northwestern along the forty-ninth parallel. The line to the head of the Mississippi had of course been found to be impossible. When the United States acquired Louisiana and became a trans-Mississippi power, the northwest boundary with British America had to be extended to the Rockies. Attempts to do so in 1803 and 1807 had failed. Now the forty-ninth parallel was adopted. It was not really an artificial boundary, but an astronomical approximation to the watershed between the waters flowing to the Gulf of Mexico and those flowing to the Arctic Ocean and Hudson Bay. The Anglo-American balance of power in America had thus projected the line partitioning the continent to the last western watershed. It failed to settle the conflicting claims of the two countries on the Pacific, and provided for joint occupation.

When even there in 1846 the partition was completed, once

more the United States received the agricultural lands and the commercial posts while British America held the fur-trade territory.[6] The astronomical boundary was extended to the Gulf of Georgia, sparing only Vancouver Island by turning down to the Strait of Juan de Fuca. The United States and British America then marched side by side from sea to sea. One half the continent north of Mexico was American, one half was British.

Such was the simple physical result. In terms of commerce, population, and power the results were very different. British America was left the country of the northern economy, the economy of the great staples of fish, fur, and timber. Habitable farm lands there were, but small in relation to the whole, enough to feed the staple trades and even to export surpluses, but not enough to support a population comparable with that so rapidly growing in the United States. Thus though a continental country, Canada was still dependent, as the northern maritime frontier had always been. Moreover, though continental in extent, it was still surprisingly maritime in character. The Atlantic islands and Acadian peninsula, the St. John, the St. Lawrence, Hudson Bay, the Saskatchewan, the Fraser, the Gulf of Georgia, it was by their sea inlets and inland waterways that British America lived.

Finally, in terms of power there could be no question of the result. British America was the residue of two bids for supremacy in America, one lost by France to Britain and the American colonies, one lost by Britain to the United States and France. Canada had survived the last trial of strength in 1812, had even had its victories, but the settlements of 1818 and the Monroe Doctrine registered the fact that supremacy in America rested with the United States.

Why then was this supremacy not translated into continental empire once again? The power and prestige of imperial Britain, secure from major commitments in Europe for a century, was a large part of the answer. Even more potent perhaps was the fact that American destiny drove westward; rarely was it tempted to

6. Norman Graebner, *Empire on the Pacific* (New York, 1958), p. 105.

turn north. The fur trade, the timber trade, the wheat lands, these could not divert Americans from the Mississippi valley, the Pacific coast and the trade of Asia. These things they wanted supremely; they did not by contrast think Canada worth the difficulty of taking. As a result, the United States realized a western destiny, and Canada was left to work out a northern one. Both countries achieved transcontinental territories: the United States in independence leading on to world power; Canada in colonial dependence leading on to self-government by evolution, to national union in cultural duality, and to independence in a set of Commonwealth and American relations of a novel kind, suggestive of much in the power systems of the nuclear age.

Chapter II

Canada in the Commonwealth

The Constitution of the Second British Empire

To Americans revolution has meant liberty. However long the preparation, whatever the richness of the inheritance of freedom from England, revolution was the means by which Americans achieved liberty. To Canadians not revolution but empire has meant liberty. Whatever the restraints empire might impose, the restraints were for the common good. However long Imperial sovereignty might endure, in the end membership in the Empire was the means by which Canadian freedom would be perfected.

That Imperial sovereignty Canadians knew operated within self-imposed limits. Not only did it rarely, except in matters of trade, legislate for a colony without its consent or to prevent a breakdown of government; it never after 1778 taxed a colony. The pledge given the American colonies when conciliation was attempted after the disaster of Saratoga, that the American colonies would not be taxed in the future, was freely extended to all the other colonies and meticulously observed.[1] Thus Canadians never had to fight a battle for no taxation without representation. The Americans had won it for them, and the Imperial parliament in the plenitude of its power respected the decision. On the contrary, what it did do year after year from 1775 to 1871 was to vote taxes to maintain the colonial governments and Imperial garrisons in British North America. In the second Empire it was the British tax payer who was finally to revolt against taxation without representation in colonial legislatures! But the consequence was that Canadians have in their history sought not liberty in independence, but self-government within the Empire.

The Winning of Self-Government Within the Empire, 1830–1848

By the reorganization which followed the War of Independence the British North American colonies enjoyed representative government as the former colonies had done. But the colonists had little control over the executive government of each colony. They lived, that is, under laws locally made, but the administration of those laws did not necessarily accord with the wishes of colonial opinion. Appointment to public office and the distribution of the patronage of government was confined to small groups of conservative colonists and permanent officials. Representative government, then, was something less than self-government. In sum, the British American colonies were given the constitution of the old royal colonies, with the position of the governors and councils strengthened against encroachment by the assembly, and brought more into line than the old had been with the stock eighteenth-century concept of a mixed constitution of monarchical, aristocratic, and democratic elements balancing in an independent executive and an independent legislature. William Pitt and his cousin William Grenville gave as full expression as possible to this concept of colonial government in the

---

1. *Statutes at Large*, XXXIII, 18 Geo. III, c. 12.

Canada Act of 1791, by which the two provinces of Lower and Upper Canada were given constitutions.

There had not been wanting voices between 1784 and 1830 to call attention to the limitations of representative government in British North America. Every colony had one or more critics who attacked, directly or by implication, the control of government by an entrenched and favoured oligarchy. But in every case outside Lower Canada before 1820, these critics fell silent, left the colony, or were suppressed by the local compact. Only in that province, with its great French majority, were these critics active and numerous enough to form a permanent opposition in the legislature. It is too little recognized that the French Canadian was the central figure in the evolution of self-government in Canada.

As opposition to the colonial governments developed before 1830, it gradually assumed in the Canadas and Nova Scotia the character of a reform movement. For reform of the colonial constitutions, rather than the passage of specific measures, became the central political issue in the Canadas and in Nova Scotia by 1830. Thus the critics of government came to be called Reformers, for like their counterparts in the United Kingdom, what they sought was the reform of the constitution itself. Gradually out of such issues as control of finance, the distribution of patronage, the legal status of American settlers, the rights of religious dissenters, the continuation of the Anglican establishment, and Anglican control of higher education, there arose a body of opinion supporting something like political parties in the three colonies. As some of the issues they agitated were also in dispute in the United Kingdom, the British immigrants, in general more liberal in their outlook than the American Canadians, greatly reenforced the movement for reform.

So great did the political agitation in the Canadas become that in 1828 it was looked into by a Select Committee of the House of Commons. Its report was generally favourable to the contentions of the Reformers. Just as the long Tory reaction in the United Kingdom was ending, so the role of the entrenched oligarchies in British North America was reaching its term. When the Whigs came into power in England in 1830, they were disposed to look favourably on the cause of colonial reform. For one thing, they hoped to reduce, or eliminate, the cost of governing dependencies like the British North American colonies, which had considerable revenues of their own. In the second place, they hoped, as in the United Kingdom, to cheapen government by making it more efficient. Finally, they sincerely, if rather vaguely, wished to put colonial government on a more popular basis.[2]

How these things were to be done was not clear. The Whigs did, however, look at the colonial governments as practical parliamentarians. What they saw disturbed them, as it seemed an unintelligent parody of government as practised in the United Kingdom. For one thing, control of revenue and expenditure had come to be divided between the assembly and the executive and the result was friction and waste. The remedy, however, was not simply to turn the control of all expenditure over to the assemblies, for those bodies might use the power of the purse to stop administration and interfere with the course of justice. The Colonial Office therefore took up a recommendation of the Select Committee of 1828, that the colonies should adopt the British practice of voting a "civil list" for the life of the sovereign. This was a fixed sum *per annum* for the payment of judicial and official salaries.

The prosaic, unimaginative measure was great in its implications. For by this and similar measures the eighteenth-century colonial constitutions might be made over step by step into the British parliamentary system of the nineteenth century. The civil list was actually a prior condition of self-government on the British model. One by one the colonies accepted the proposal, except the Assembly of Lower Canada. The French majority

2. Helen Taft Manning, "The Colonial Policy of the Whig Ministers, 1830–47": I, *Canadian Historical Review*, Sept., 1952, pp. 203–6; II, *ibid.*, Dec. 1952, pp. 341–68.

there could not see themselves surrendering the only control they had over the English members of the Executive Council and, moreover, paying those gentlemen a fixed salary for an indefinite period.

For this and other reasons the course to self-government was not to run smoothly across the stepping-stones of Whig administrative measures. What the colonial Reformers wanted, and their desires were inflamed by the triumphs of Jacksonian democracy, the July Revolution, and the passage of the Reform Bill, was control of the colonial executive government on some comprehensive system or principle. From the agitation in the Canadas two proposals for such a system emerged.

One was a logical development of the existing constitutions, but it was wholly democratic and partly American in inspiration. It was the "elective system" advocated by Louis Joseph Papineau, the French leader of the Lower Canadian Reformers, and his radical followers, both French and English. It was also favoured by the more radical Reformers of Upper Canada. These Reformers proposed at this time no more than that the Legislative Council should be made elective, for that was the body which threw out their bills, but the proposal pointed directly to the election of the governor also. The proposal was therefore criticized by some as being republican and American.[3]

The other proposal, however, was parliamentary and British. It was that there should be "responsible government" in the colonies. By that its proposers, Dr. W. W. Baldwin and his son Robert, meant that the Executive Council should be made up of members of the local legislature and that they should answer as a body to the legislature for their conduct of the government of the colony. It was a proposal which had the simplicity of genius. Few, however, were equipped to understand it in the colonies, and in the United Kingdom the instant reaction was that it was incom-

3. The proposal of elective institutions was of course partly inspired by the British Radicals, but it was American example the Canadian Reformers turned to increasingly before 1837.

patible with Imperial control of the colony. Moreover, "responsible government" was a term of many meanings, ranging from individual executive ministers being subject to impeachment to members of the legislature being responsible because elected. And in any event there could be no cabinet government in British America until the framework and functioning of government were bit by bit made over to allow it. For the existing colonial governments were much more congressional than parliamentary in their constitution and operation.

In consequence, the more radical Canadian Reformers did not generally accept the Baldwinian proposal, but endorsed the elective system. Such a course meant a clash with the Whig program of piecemeal adoption of British parliamentary usage, and in 1837 the mounting grievances of Lower Canada flared into rebellion under the sting of Lord John Russell's invoking the overriding authority of the Imperial parliament to pay the official salaries the Assembly had refused to vote. The rebellion in Lower Canada was American in both inspiration and conduct. *Les patriotes* voted non-consumption; counties resolved and confederated; *les Fils de la Liberté* armed. And if republics of Lower and Upper Canada, where the radicals under William Lyon Mackenzie also rose, had established themselves, it may be supposed that they would have followed Texas into the Union. But British regulars and loyal militia and volunteers soon scattered the ill-organized and scantily-supported risings. Canadian reform was not to move through revolution to elective and republican institutions. That path had not only been blocked; it had been rejected by a majority of Canadians, French as well as English.

The rebellions, none the less, made the "Canadian question" of leading importance in British politics for the only time in Canadian history. For the first time a top-rank politician was sent to deal with Canadian affairs in the person of Lord Durham. Durham recommended that the Canadas should be united in order to swamp the French with an English majority, and that responsible government as the Baldwins had defined it should then be granted to the colonies. He saw clearly that Canadians could not be left with antiquated institutions beside the United States. They must either have American institutions or British ones. Provided the French did not constitute a majority in Canada, Durham thought the colonies must be given self-government by means of British parliamentary institutions. He was quite confident this could be done within the Empire; it was only necessary, he declared, for the Imperial government to retain control of foreign affairs, trade, the colonial constitutions, and the public lands.

Durham's confidence was not shared by the Whig government or Lord John Russell, its Colonial Secretary. Russell did indeed sponsor an Act of Parliament which united the Canadas in 1840, but he did not grant responsible government to Canada or the other colonies. Instead he sent a brilliant parliamentarian and administrator, Poulett Thomson, later Lord Sydenham, to manage the new Canadian government. In effect, Russell had continued the old Whig policy of making over the colonial constitutions. By the Act uniting the Canadas, for example, it was made statutory that a money bill could be introduced only on the recommendation of a minister of the Crown. This of course was one of the pivotal conventions of parliamentary government, that on which the whole system of budgetary control of expenditure rests.

Members of the executive council, moreover, were henceforth to hold office at the governor's pleasure. As a matter of practice, they were also chosen from that time on only from among the membership of the legislatures. The changes were meant at once to free the governor from the old official cliques and to establish harmony between him and the assembly. Sydenham and his successors, however, refused to appoint their councils solely from any one group in the legislature, and deliberately denied the colonies the last characteristic of cabinet government, that it is normally also party government. Much friction followed these refusals in Canada and Nova Scotia from 1841 to 1846.

Then suddenly the whole context of colonial self-government was transformed by the repeal of the Corn Laws. This commercial revolution, one of the same order of magnitude in the second Empire as the American Revolution was in the first, meant that the United Kingdom in replacing its mercantile policies by free trade had emancipated itself from its colonies, and particularly those in North America. There was no longer need to insist on the superintending sovereignty of the Colonial Office and the Imperial parliament. Suddenly the ideas of the colonial Reformers, of Charles Buller and Lord Grey in England, of Robert Baldwin and Joseph Howe in Canada and Nova Scotia, found all opposition ended. Party ministries were formed and colonial governors ceased to be active executives and began to study the conventions of constitutional monarchy. Indeed, such was the eagerness of the Imperial government that responsible government was not only granted to those colonies which desired it; it was pressed upon those which were indifferent, such as New Brunswick.

The commercial revolution of 1846 did not of course mark the end of the second Empire. The Empire was rather changed from one resting on mercantile control and parliamentary sovereignty to one evolving in self-government with a common heritage of freedom symbolized by allegiance to the Crown. The United Kingdom had discarded the doubtful profits of empire, but continued to acknowledge the moral trust and many obligations of imperial rule. The self-governing colonies, having achieved their goal of self-government by adapting British institutions to local needs, had no desire to sever the connection with the United Kingdom. Indeed they insisted on retaining it, for to them the Empire had become an empire of constitutional example and patriotic sentiment. They were, they protested, British in feeling and in mode of government.

From this dual triumph of liberal Imperial policy and Canadian responsible government two consequences were to follow. One was the realization of liberty in empire by the extension of colonial self-government. The other was the rise on the basis of self-government of colonial nationhood. The British American quest for self-government within the Empire had thus supplied the fundamental elements of the present Commonwealth, the free association of independent nations.

The Formation of the Dominion, 1850–1885

By the Declaration of Independence Americans consciously resolved to be "a separate and equal" nation among the nations of the world. In achieving self-government, Canadians all unwittingly had set out to be an associated, but equal, nation within the British Empire. No explicit formulation was given to this determination; its revelation was left to the working of time and event. But in responsible government, perhaps Irish in inspiration, certainly Canadian in formulation, and largely British in implementation, Canadians attained to what has proved to be their only achievement of more than Canadian significance. For responsible government was to prove to be not only the mode of devolution of self-government upon British colonies; it has also been the method of peaceful transfer of sovereignty from the Empire to the peoples of India and British Africa. That what was worked out on the banks of the St. Lawrence and the shores of Lake Ontario should have helped, however remotely, to bring into being great new states of free and sovereign communities on the banks of the Ganges and the Indus and on the coasts of West and East Africa, constitutes Canada's single but significant contribution to the slow elaboration of human freedom.

It could prove to be so because colonial self-government was not a condition but a process. Durham's easy formulation of the subjects to be reserved for Imperial control was as easily eroded by the ever-advancing claims of the colonies to ever more powers of self-government. Only a rigid federal constitution might have stayed the process, and for such a constitution neither the British nor the colonists had any desire. Much more percipient was Durham's other statement that for success colonial self-government would require "some nationality of his own" on the part of the colonist.[4] Such was precisely the effect responsible government was to have; it helped both to create and to express a growing sense of that paradox, colonial nationality.

Under the liberal institutions of the Empire, such a process was inevitable. Canadians used their new powers of self-government to create Canadian institutions. In Upper Canada they separated church and state; in Lower Canada they strengthened the semi-establishment of the Roman Catholic Church which the Quebec Act had created. Out of the difference arose that Canadian phenomenon, the separate school, the denominational school supported by public funds. They likewise incorporated the ecclesiastical corporations of Lower Canada. They made municipal government democratic. They abolished *seigneurial* tenure in Lower Canada, buying out the *seigneurs*. They abolished primogeniture in Upper Canada. They made the Legislative Council elective. They codified the civil law of Lower Canada. In short, in a conservative and relative way, they created in Canada the liberal and democratic institutions of the nineteenth century. The Atlantic provinces followed at a slower pace. What at bottom Canadian society is today, it was made in the first decade after the granting of responsible government.

It is true that the same decade was the first great era of continental attraction to the United States in Canadian history since the final loss of the old Southwest in 1814. The St. Lawrence canals of the era and the Grand Trunk Railway were designed to draw the traffic of the American Midwest to the St. Lawrence. The Reciprocity Treaty of 1854 was meant to find in America the markets lost in the Empire by the commercial revolution of 1846. The degree of continental involvement was symbolized by Canada replacing a sterling currency by a dollar one.

The era of continental attraction did little, however, to check the growth of national feeling. By 1858 two Canadian publicists, one the English Alexander Morris, one the French Joseph Charles Taché, both names of note in Canada, were calling for the union

4. Sir Charles Lucas (ed.), *Lord Durham's Report on the Affairs of British North America, II* (Oxford, 1912), p. 311.

of all British North America and the creation of what Morris called "a northern nationality."[5] The proposition was one demanding serious consideration. For one thing, the Canadian union was being worked with ever greater friction and effort. Intended as an attempt to assimilate the French, it had been defeated by the grant of responsible government which the French used to defend and entrench their institutions. An incomplete union in that it left French civil law untouched and gave separate and equal representation to Lower and Upper Canada, the union had failed to provide a plural society with a satisfactory government. Increasingly the assembly tended to divide into sectional blocs, steadily the legislation for one section tended to be passed or blocked by the votes of the other. The principle of majority rule will work only in a society which is fairly homogeneous in composition; when the society is insufficiently homogeneous, majority rule becomes, or is resented as, an instrument of oppression. Unless some new frame of government were adopted, parliamentary government in Canada would deadlock, whatever the growth of national sentiment.

At the same time there was a growing feeling that British North America would be well advised to seek means of commercial and strategic union. Since 1836 there had been talk of an intercolonial railway from the Atlantic provinces to Canada. Such a railway would give Canada winter ports and the eastern provinces a new market. It would also allow the British garrisons in Canada to be re-enforced in winter. It might even aid Canada's giant but sickly railway, the Grand Trunk, to gain a little strength.

The intercolonial railway and the union of British America were old themes. But an even older one, not heard of for many years, was that of the extension of Canada to the Red and Saskatchewan rivers and even to the Pacific. In 1857 an inquiry into the Hudson's Bay Company's administration of its vast territories, the

5. Alexander Morris, *The Hudson's Bay and Pacific Territories* (Montreal, 1859), reprinted in *Nova Britannia* (Toronto, 1884); Joseph Charles Taché, *Des Provinces de l'Amérique du Nord et d'une union fédérale* (Quebec, 1858).

end of good land in Canada West, and the discovery of gold on the Fraser River, started an agitation for the acquisition of the Northwest by Canada.

All these projects were given point and unity when in 1858 the Canadian government proposed a federation of British North America. It was a sudden, ill-matured proposal which sprang from Canadian political exigencies rather than due consideration. The Colonial Secretary of the day was irritated at not being consulted, the governors of the Atlantic provinces thought the union of those provinces should be the first step, the French were dubious about adding to Canada West, the Hudson's Bay Company had still to be bought out. Finally, the great depression of 1857 took the drive out of every project in Canada and elsewhere. The union of British North America had to await a stronger conjunction of events.

Six years later all the elements of 1858 were still at work, but one new and catastrophic had been added, the American Civil War. That conflict posed drastic possibilities not only for the American Union, but also for the whole continent. British Americans at first, thinking the war one to abolish slavery, in the majority favoured the North. When it became evident it was a war to preserve the Union, the pro-Northern sentiment diminished. Many still favoured the North; it may be that the number of pro-Southerners did not greatly increase. Undoubtedly, however, the general Canadian feeling became anti-Northern.[6] This attitude of course aroused American resentment towards British America during and after the war. As Canadians and other British Americans watched the struggle, they realized that a victory for the North would mean a stronger and perhaps a more aggressive Union in which the check on expansion into free soil by the South would be removed. They feared that American anti-British feeling might end the Reciprocity Treaty. They knew that in some quarters of the North there was a positive desire to annex the

6. Cf. Robin B. Winks, *Canada and the United States: the Civil War Years* (Baltimore, 1960), chap. 11.

British provinces. To face dangers so great, if undefined, a union was obviously desirable.

When therefore political deadlock occurred in the Canadian Union and the Atlantic provinces proposed to discuss a Maritime union, the Canadian government suggested a meeting to discuss the union of all British America. The initiative was Canadian, but the Maritimers readily agreed. Moreover, the Imperial government, painfully aware since the Trent affair of 1861 that the American war might in one way or another result in a conflict with the United States, was positively resolved that the union of British America should be accomplished as a preparation for the lessening, if not the end, of imperial commitments in America.

So impelled, the Fathers of Confederation met promptly, and produced quickly a scheme of union. It was not, properly speaking, a federal union, but a legislative one with concessions as limited as possible to safeguard the particular rights of the French. The proposed constitution was not federal, although it allowed a federal interpretation being put upon it. Its essential legislative character meant that it was not an imitation of the American Union, not even one that avoided the faults which were then thought to have brought the disruption of that Union in 1861. The proposed scheme of government was, the Fathers insisted, a union monarchical in principle, parliamentary in form, and traditional in spirit. "We consulted the oracles of history and our race," said D'Arcy McGee, the orator of Confederation.[7] But above all it was an attempt to create in British America a new nation which should be, in Macdonald's phrase, "a subordinate kingdom" in the Empire.

The union of British America was, after modifications of the Quebec plan and serious delays in the Maritimes, accepted in

7. Peter B. Waite, "Ideas and Politics in British North America, 1864–1866" (Unpublished Ph.D. Thesis, University of Toronto, 1953), p. 1. (Mr. Waite's study will shortly be published by the University of Toronto Press under the title *The Life and Times of Confederation, 1864–1867*.)

principle by the legislatures of Canada, New Brunswick, and
Nova Scotia, and in the spring of 1867 was ratified by the Imperial parliament. "We are laying the foundations of a great
state," declared the Colonial Secretary, Lord Carnarvon, intro-
ducing the British North America Bill, "perhaps one which at a
future day may even overshadow this country. But, come what
may, we shall rejoice that we have shown neither indifference to
their wishes nor jealousy of their aspirations, but that we hon-
estly and sincerely, to the utmost of our power, fostered their
growth, recognizing in it the conditions of our own greatness."[8]

The new nation in the Empire was launched on July 1, 1867.
Its first Prime Minister, Sir John Macdonald, had emerged as
the unifier of British America and as one of the four great unifiers
of the century. He did not possess the infinite capacity to suffer
which was Lincoln's, or the force of Bismarck, or the subtlety of
Cavour. But he did have in full measure the ultimate political
capacity to await the event in its time, to turn it to a purpose
long nourished, and to work through the confusion and frustra-
tion of the political warfare of a clamorous democracy to the
realization of a design clearly seen and strongly held. Macdonald
proposed to make a nation on the northern half of the continent
which, as a member of the Empire, would perpetuate British
institutions in America for all time to come.

Under his leadership the first Canadian cabinet set itself to
build the Intercolonial Railway to link the Atlantic provinces
with those of the St. Lawrence. It acquired in 1870 the Hudson's
Bay territory which ranged from Labrador to the Rockies. In
1871 it brought British Columbia into the Union. A Pacific railway was then undertaken by a nation with fewer people than
the state of Wisconsin today. And when in 1871 the outstanding
issues between the British Empire and the United States were
disposed of in the Treaty of Washington, what Canadians could
read between the lines was that the continental drive of the

8. Great Britain, *House of Lords Debates,* 3rd series, vol. 185, p. 576-b.

United States had at last been contained. It was well that it was so, for in 1871 the British garrisons went home. The two transcontinental states marched parallel from sea to sea, the independent republic holding the hegemony of the Americas, the subordinate kingdom a colony yet a nation, self-governing yet part of the Empire of which it was in fact the residuary legatee in America. In one the tradition of revolutionary and independent liberty was embodied in republican and democratic institutions. In the other the British tradition of evolving freedom was transmitted in the ancient institutions of monarchy and parliament. True to their original characters, the republic's institutions had the classic symmetry and the perfection of the Enlightenment, those of the subordinate kingdom the foundation and the lift of Victorian Gothic.[9]

Canada in 1871 was, however, a nation projected rather than a nation formed. To build on the basis of the northern economy, within a world empire, under the influence of a dynamic neighbour, at once alien and kin, in such circumstances to build a nation out of two peoples of two cultures without the compulsion of war or revolution, was an undertaking of unique dimensions and unprecedented conditions. It is not to be wondered at that the achievement of the project was slow. The young men of the Canada First movement might complain at the lack of a national spirit and claim that only independence could kindle the flame by which nations were forged. The great depression of 1873 checked the impetus of nation-building that had carried Canada to the Pacific. Yet the work went on. Somehow the shaky fabric held through the bitter years of the mid-seventies and at the end came the National Policy of tariff protection which was to guarantee the industrial strength to complete the Pacific railway. In 1885 the line was finished, every foot on

9. The fancy may perhaps be pursued further: the Capitol at Washington houses the essential anarchy of American congressional politics; the Victorian Gothic of Ottawa, the Benthamite efficiency of the Canadian Civil Service.

Canadian soil from the Ottawa around the cliffs and inlets of Superior's North Shore, and across the prairies to the passes of the Rockies and the Fraser's gorge. What had been inked in on the maps had been laid out on the ground in rock and iron. British capital and American skill had been harnessed by Canadian purpose to make the northern nation of Morris and the subordinate kingdom of Macdonald one of the operating facts of the British Empire and the American continent. The principle of self-government within the Empire now had acquired the material weight to become the principle of autonomous nationhood in the comity of nations.

The Canadian Nation in the British Empire, 1885–1917

The development of Canadian nationhood from the colonial self-government of 1848 to the continental stature of 1871 was not only a matter of Canadian growth. It was also a result of Imperial policy. In that period the colonial policy of the United Kingdom was liberal. In general, that is, it looked to the day when the colonies of settlement, increased in strength and practised in self-government, would swing out into national orbits of their own, attached still, it was hoped, by ties of allegiance and affection to the mother country. The economic liberals, such as John Bright, Robert Lowe, and Goldwin Smith indeed thought the process should be quickened by paternal pressure, for they suspected the colonies of seeking to combine a maximum of self-government with a maximum of imperial aid.

With respect to Canada, there was another and more compelling factor than liberal principles afforded. That was the strategic necessity of the Empire not being committed to war or a show of strength in America when its resources were required to maintain the balance of power in Europe. Only Canada seemed likely to lead to danger of such a commitment in America. This fact had been driven home in 1864 when Bismarck began the unification of Germany, and the British resolve to complete Confederation and withdraw its garrisons owed much to the rise of modern

Germany. The last troops sailed from Quebec in 1871 while German forces still occupied the soil of France.

The same events, however, were to change the attitude of English statesmen towards the Empire. As is so often noted, Disraeli's wretched millstones of 1852 became props of England's imperial might in 1872. The first stages of the change were actually the work of colonials, or Englishmen with interests in the colonies, who formed the Royal Colonial Institute in 1871. But it was only as England faced the facts of the industrialization of a united Germany and a reunited United States in the economic depression of the 1880's, that English statesmen generally began to see in the once little-valued colonies the population and resources which might enable the United Kingdom to match her new trade rivals. As a result, the Imperial Federation League was formed in 1884 to seek ways of co-ordinating the economic and military resources of the United Kingdom and its colonies. It was not the intent of the founders of the League to go back on what had been done between 1848 and 1871. They hoped that they might, however, bring colonial self-government into some defined working relationship with the United Kingdom in commerce and strategy.

It was then a somewhat different climate from that in which colonial self-government had flourished that Canadian national development was to go forward. But as the new climate was still liberal, that development did go forward, and pretty much at the pace Canadians desired.

Canadians began, with British credentials, to represent Canada on special missions to Washington, Macdonald in 1871, his great rival, George Brown, in 1874. When an active and flamboyant Governor General, Lord Dufferin, acted more like an imperial viceroy than a constitutional monarch, his ministers had his successors' instructions altered so as to make it quite clear that the Governor General acted in all Canadian matters only on his ministers' advice. A Supreme Court was erected, having final jurisdiction in all criminal cases. The protective tariff of 1879,

while directed against American goods, gave no explicit concession to those of the United Kingdom. A High Commissioner
was appointed to represent the Canadian government in London
in 1879, and it became the practice to associate him with the negotiation of commercial treaties in which Canada had a direct
interest.

In all this Canada was advancing its national self-interests
within the Imperial framework. There was at first little sentiment
in the development. How little sentiment might affect Canadian
policy was illustrated when in 1884 Prime Minister Macdonald
declined to send a Canadian expeditionary force to the Sudan
for the relief of Gordon. National interest was the prime criterion
of Canadian policy. But the Imperial Federation League began
to work in Canada in 1885, Canadian volunteers in British pay
did serve on the Nile, and a popular imperialist sentiment did
began to build up in English Canada, particularly in response to
the fierce *nationalisme* touched off in Quebec when Louis Riel
was hanged for leading the half-breed and Indian rising on the
Saskatchewan.

At first the new sentiment affected only local and domestic
politics. It was national interest alone which guided Canada between the Scylla and Charybdis of commercial union with the
United States in the election of 1891 and of imperial preference
with the United Kingdom after 1896. In 1897 the budget did
provide a tariff preference on British imports, but no imperial
preference was sought in return.

It was not possible thereafter to keep *nationaliste* and imperialist feeling out of the development of Canadian relations
within the Empire. In the Boer War the government of Sir Wilfrid Laurier was caught squarely between a reluctance, voiced by
the French Canadian *nationalistes* but not felt by them alone, to
participate in an "imperialist" war, and a resolution, strongest
among the old British stock, that Canada should participate. A
compromise was found in sending two small contingents which
served under British command with British pay. But issues had

been drawn which it might not be possible to compromise in a greater struggle.

Nor was it only contending sentiments that made the path of Canadian government difficult as Canada entered the twentieth century. The two jubilees of Queen Victoria had given rise to the Colonial Conference, and in those of 1897, 1902, and 1907, Canada was pressed to consider the creation of an Imperial Council to formulate the policies of the Empire, the adoption of a system of imperial preference and the contribution of money or ships to the Royal Navy. To all these proposals Laurier answered no. It was not merely Canadian intransigence, still less French Canadian. There could in fact be no other answer. The die of responsible government had been cast in 1848. The colonial prime ministers headed national governments answerable to national parliaments and democratic electorates.

Canada therefore refused to entertain the idea of an Imperial Council, or to lessen its control of tariff policy by reciprocal imperial preferences, or to contribute to the Royal Navy. But the imperialist elements in Canada challenged this decision, and when the naval race between England and Germany became critical in 1908, their pressure forced the government's hand. It responded to the joint pressures of national and imperial sentiment by the establishment of a Canadian navy which might in emergency be placed under the command of the British Admiralty. The compromise satisfied neither extreme of sentiment. In 1911 Laurier was defeated by the imperialist vote of English Canada which voted against reciprocity with the United States which might draw Canada into the Union, and the *nationaliste* vote of Quebec which voted against a Canadian navy which might serve in an imperialist war.

The lessons of the period from the election of 1891 to the defeat of Laurier seem clear enough now. Canada, placed between American continentalism and British imperialism, had to keep control of tariff policy and yield to neither extreme of commercial union or imperial preference, lest either complicate its commercial and political relations with the Empire or the Republic. It had similarly to limit military or naval commitments to the Empire, not only because of a deep isolationist sentiment, strongest in Quebec but strong elsewhere, but also because it was evident since the Venezuelan crisis of 1895 that Canada's strategic relations had entered a new and uncertain stage. That crisis had led to the planning of a mobilization of the Canadian militia. Yet it was obvious that the United Kingdom would not allow such a crisis to develop again. Protected by the Monroe Doctrine against every power but the United States, Canada, it seemed, would do best to keep its hands free and develop its economy. Only one thing would move Canada to military action in the Empire, a major war which threatened the Empire as a whole. And participation in such a war, thanks to the American friendship won by the withdrawal of British power from America, would arouse no opposition from the United States. Finally, only a national sovereignty of unquestionable validity could mediate between French Canadian *nationalisme* and British imperialist sentiment. Thus it was that the years of the Laurier regime saw the rise of a Canadian national spirit, neither French nor British but wholly Canadian in sentiment. It was a compromise, but a powerful compromise in that it attempted to reconcile strong extremes, and in that, though powerful, it was essentially moderate. It was, in short, Canadian, the characteristic product of a country resting on paradoxes and anomalies, governed only by compromise and kept strong only by moderation.

Canada had then to realize further within the Empire that sense of nationality the practice of self-government had created, even if the realization meant a refashioning of the Empire itself. The process was immensely quickened and sharpened by the First World War. When the United Kingdom declared war in 1914 the whole Empire was at war. But it was for Canada to determine the degree of its participation. It was free to do so; the United Kingdom had no power to raise a man or a shilling in Canada. Nor was there any internal opposition. The German violation of Belgian neutrality and the threat to the United Kingdom itself unified Canada. It was recognized everywhere that this transcended the colonial wars of the past.

As the war sagged into the stalemate on the western front, however, the Canadian military effort exceeded all that anyone had anticipated. By 1916 there could be no question of Canadian forces fighting dispersed under British command. National sentiment and responsible government forbade. A Canadian Corps was created and given a Canadian commander in General Arthur Currie. It was essential that the Canadian government should be able to answer to the parliament and people of Canada for the disposition and use of the Canadian forces. The necessity was recognized by no one as strongly as the Canadian government of the day, the government elected in 1911 by imperialist and *nationaliste* votes.

It was to meet this need, felt by the other Dominions no less than Canada, that the Imperial War Cabinet was devised in 1917 to give the Dominions and India a voice in the making of policy for the war and the peace. The War Cabinet proved to be only a device which failed to become an institution, but its inception marked the beginning of the transformation of the Empire into the Commonwealth. The practice of self-government had resulted in national autonomy within the British Empire which was already being called the Commonwealth, and after the war the constitutional relations of the Empire would have to be readjusted accordingly, such readjustments to "... be based upon a full recognition of the Dominions as autonomous nations of an Imperial Commonwealth, and of India as an important portion of the same. ... "

The Evolution of the Commonwealth, 1917–1959

By the Declaration of the Imperial Conference of 1917 the Commonwealth was founded in principle. But at the same time it entered on a new phase of evolution. Much had still to be done to give the new nations the functions appropriate to their status.

And it had also to be determined whether the War Cabinet would become an agency of policy-making in peace time.

The admission of the Dominion delegations to the Peace Conference in their own right, actually if not formally, and to the League of Nations without qualification, did much to equate function with status, and launched the Dominions into international affairs as separate and sovereign entities.

The idea of an Imperial Cabinet, however, had short shrift. When at the Conference of 1921 the Dominions were allowed a voice in policy-making, the Prime Minister of Canada, Mr. Arthur Meighen, used the occasion to be the voice of America and persuaded the United Kingdom, against the opposition of Australia, not to renew the Anglo-Japanese Treaty which was causing resentment in the United States. The Imperial Cabinet and adequate voice might have survived even this prophetic use, had it not been that in 1921 Mr. W. L. Mackenzie King won the general election of that year with the whole Quebec representation of sixty-five behind him, and with sixty-five almost equally isolationist Progressives from Ontario and the prairies to conciliate. When therefore the impetuous Mr. Churchill threatened Turkey with war against the might of the whole British Empire, Prime Minister King let it be known in London that Canada would not be committed to war by any act of the United Kingdom. The Chanak affair, as it was called, ended any prospect there may have been of the Commonwealth developing any central body to turn consultation into policy-making. Even the concept of an Imperial Cabinet of prime ministers each responsible to his parliament, satisfying as it seemed in theory, had not sufficed to overcome the attitudes created by the practice of self-government and the growth of colonial nationalism. In the Conference of 1923 Prime Minister King made his views prevail.[10]

It remained only for the Conference of 1926 to recognize the

10. R. M. Dawson, *William Lyon Mackenzie King* (Toronto, 1958), pp. 478–80.

situation which the national intransigence of Canada, the Irish Free State, and the Union of South Africa had created. The Declaration of that year proclaimed that the members of the Commonwealth were equal in status and freely associated, and that the remaining disparities between status and functions should be removed. The details were worked out for the Conference of 1930, which approved the draft of the Statute of Westminster, 1931.

Then, by a last act of sovereignty the Parliament of the United Kingdom, at the request of the Dominions, declared that the imperial sovereignty maintained so hardly against the Americans in 1776 was at an end in the Dominions. Only the Crown remained to connect the nations of the Commonwealth, and thereafter, even in the appointment of his personal representative, the Governor General, the King acted only on the advice of the Cabinet of the Dominion concerned.

It seemed a clean and conclusive end to imperial sovereignty and for the Irish Free State and South Africa it was. Australia and New Zealand were doubtful of the merits of the change and did not ratify the Statute for some years. Canada, because its governments could not agree on how to amend the national-provincial sections of the British North America Act, had had those parts of the Act explicitly excluded from the operation of the Statute, and to this day must go to Westminster to have the national-provincial sections of its constitution amended.

In principle, however, the Statute of Westminster was conclusive. The British Dominions had become sovereign nations in law as in fact. Much, it is true, remained to be settled. As the Crown was now the only legal tie within the Commonwealth, how was the succession to be determined, could a Dominion secede, could a Dominion be neutral when the Crown was at war? The legal and political pundits spun many fine arguments around the divisibility or indivisibility of the Crown. One by one the questions were settled practically. The abdication crisis of 1936 pointed up the fact that there could be more than one monarch in the Commonwealth at the same time, though none thought it desirable. The Free State seceded to become a republic in 1937,[11] and no on said it nay. And in 1939 Canada remained at peace, and presumably neutral, for one week after the United Kingdom had declared war on Germany.

Nevertheless the war revealed that the free association of the Commonwealth did allow co-operation in a unity which stood the severest test of war. For over a year the Commonwealth, greatly aided by the known friendship of the United States, stood alone against a Europe dominated by triumphant Germany.

Even so, Canadians could not but wonder whether the Commonwealth and Empire had not run its course and exhausted its significance. When the war was over the United Nations rather than the Commonwealth seemed to many Canadians the new association in which the Commonwealth nations would find their natural orbits. That body contained the United States, now at last exercising that leadership in the world so many Canadians had wished it to assume before 1941. The Empire of the United Kingdom was rapidly moving towards dissolution, though a dissolution not caused so much by defeat in war or weakness in peace as by the operation of those same liberal principles which had led to the formation of the British Commonwealth. In Canada it was therefore felt that the great test of whether the Commonwealth had a role still to play depended on what decision the great, historic nation of India would make when it achieved independence.

When India and the other Asian Dominions, with the exception of Burma, declared in 1949 their intention to remain within the Commonwealth, there was immense satisfaction in Canada. The decision meant that the Commonwealth was not merely a matter of British sentiment, but an association founded on principles universally valid, to which nations of one of the most ancient civilizations of the world, despite two centuries of dependence, thought it important to adhere. India, Pakistan, Ceylon were warmly wel-

11. A republic in fact, though not in name, and until 1949 in "external association" with the Crown; N. Mansergh, *Survey of British Commonwealth Affairs, 1939–1952* (London, 1958), pp. 262–63.

comed to the Commonwealth and are now potent and influential members of a free association which at its best transcends differences of race and culture.

There followed easily the proclamation of the King as Head of the Commonwealth made up of republics as well as kingdoms, and at the accession of Elizabeth II the final assumption of the older Dominions of the style of "Realm." Canada at last became the Kingdom the Fathers of Confederation intended in 1867. Full sovereignty, continued co-operation, free association, such were the characteristics of the Commonwealth to which Ghana, Malaya, and Nigeria have since been welcomed, without the loss of South Africa, and to which newer members yet will be admitted, should they so desire.

The recent tragedy at Sharpeville in the Union of South Africa, of course, brings to the fore an issue long latent in Commonwealth relations. Is racial discrimination, carried to the length it is in the Union, compatible with membership in the Commonwealth? The answer offered here is no. As the chief significance of the Commonwealth is its multi-racial character, the continuance of South Africa within the Commonwealth, without a serious and progressive modification of the policy of *apartheid,* would be impossible. A policy of progressive racial discrimination is incompatible with the character of the Commonwealth since 1949, in a way a republican form of government, or even a non-democratic one, is not.

It must be said that to the interested observer there could not but occur, as the transformation of the Commonwealth took place with the resounding phrases of the new royal style, the question, was this only the dissolution of something every one had understood, whether with respect or hate, the old British Empire which had kept the Pax Britannica for the world's most peaceful and progressive century? Was that imperial might and majesty merely evaporating peacefully in a cloud of polysyllabics, to the accompaniment of amiable gestures and pleased exclamations? Could the Commonwealth continue as the implications of the national citizenship adopted by Canada in 1946 worked themselves out? Could a Commonwealth, of which the ties were not only political but also social, survive the admixture of republics and monarchies which the admission of India and the later republics initiated, when monarchy is not merely a political form, but in subtle and profound nuances a peculiar kind of society and community?[12] Only the future can answer.

There at present the matter rests. A Canadian is perhaps not the best commentator on the Commonwealth, for he is likely to see its evolution as a victory of Canadian experience. But a Canadian may say that the Commonwealth can only be left to the working of that evolution in freedom from which it rose and of the principle of free association by which it lives. It may be that the Commonwealth has realized the ideal Burke uttered in urging reconciliation with America. Its trust is in "ties light as air, but as strong as links of iron," mutual respect, mutual tolerance, co-operation where co-operation is possible, understanding where it is not. It may be that this will not amount to a great deal in terms of material power. But even if the Sidney Smith resolution of the Commonwealth Economic Conference of September, 1958, calling for the establishment of a thousand reciprocal Commonwealth scholarships, a resolution of which the application was worked out by the Commonwealth Conference on Education at Oxford in July, 1959, is all that the Commonwealth can achieve, even this is much. For ultimately only ideas prevail; ultimately men cannot be moved except they be persuaded; ultimately freedom alone unites mankind.

12. See Mansergh, *British Commonwealth Affairs, 1939–1952*, pp. 374–75, 382–87.

Chapter III

Canada and the United States

The Years of American Scepticism, 1871–1926

It has not been easy for the government or people of the United States to accept the fact of Canadian nationhood in America. The evolution of a colony to national independence by the practice of self-government within an empire ran counter to American experience and to fundamental assumptions of American historical thought. The British North American provinces were always, and of course rightly, seen and treated as colonies of the British Empire. In American belief, colonies, however, if not exploited and tyrannized over, were in constant danger of exploitation and tyranny. It followed that all colonies naturally desired to be liberated from imperial control. It was difficult therefore for Americans in general to believe that the British provincials in general neither felt exploited nor desired to be liberated. When some of them did so feel and desire in the rebellions of 1837, nothing was more inevitable than that American popular sentiment should rally to assist the work of liberation.

There was also the deeply felt and wholly amiable belief that all America was to be American. If British power checked the infiltration and prodding that might have helped the benevolent advance of Manifest Destiny in British America, the very confidence that that destiny was not only manifest but inevitable made Americans content to await the day when the British had other occupation and British Americans would rush to embrace the good fortune America had reserved for them. This confidence must be reckoned as one of the major factors that account for the survival of Canada in America.

Then too, American experience taught that colonies achieved liberty through revolution. The Canadian attainment of national autonomy by evolution in self-government was not something Americans had thought possible or indeed even desirable. The slow, pragmatic approach seemed to palter with the sacred character of liberty.

As a result, Americans tended to see,[1] as they may still do,[2] the structure of Canadian politics as that of the domination of the country's government and economy by a small, influential, pro-British group which by indoctrination and pressure kept Canada from finding its true destiny in union with the United States. In this view they were fortified by the existence from 1775 on of small groups of annexationists and republicans, by a considerable body of opinion which felt that ultimately continental union was inevitable, and, finally, by a large body of careless good nature, or even mistaken courtesy, which sometimes led considerable numbers of Canadians to say that they would welcome union with the United States. In short, Americans have always been prone to discount colonial loyalty, both French and English, to the Empire and the reality of Canadian national sentiment.

Because of this basic misunderstanding, Americans extended

1. Fish Correspondence (United States National Archives), Geo. A. Matile to Carl Schurz, July 30, 1870, forwarded to Fish, Aug. 1, 1870.
2. Joseph Barber, *Good Fences Make Good Neighbors* (New York, 1958), p. 265.

no cordial welcome to the British American union of 1867. They were, indeed, in no mood to do so because of more immediate misunderstandings and positive resentments arising out of the Civil War. There was a strong body of opinion in the United States which felt that British sympathy with the Confederacy had gone beyond anything required by law or justified by the issues of the war, and that it had prolonged the war. Much the same body of opinion felt that Canadians too had sympathized with the South and that the colonial governments had been deliberately slack in maintaining their neutrality. There had in fact been much anti-Northern feeling in British America and a good deal of official incompetence in upholding the neutral status of the colonies. Among leading American politicians like Charles Sumner, there was also a direct and familiar knowledge of the Little England sentiment in the United Kingdom. They knew that a considerable and influential party in England would not be displeased if the British American colonies joined the Republic on liberal terms.

This resentment and this knowledge led to the demand that British America be ceded to the United States in settlement of the Alabama claims and in order to end the friction that the existence of the colonies caused, a friction bound to be increased with the ending of the Reciprocity Treaty. The cry for annexation was taken up by two active pressure groups. One was made of certain New England interests which saw Canadian annexation as a way of turning New York's flank and drawing western trade through Canada to New England ports. The other was the business interests of St. Paul, Minnesota, which hoped to capture the whole of the trade of northwestern British America.

Between 1865 and 1871 the annexation cry seemed to be a formidable one, but its importance was in fact much exaggerated. For one thing, the British government quietly refused to turn over colonies without their consent as pawns to settle a claim for damages. For another, American opinion generally was certain that Confederation had been engineered by a pro-British group of politicians and carried by British pressure, and that as it did not rest on popular support, it must collapse when the British pressure was removed. Then, they were confident, the disillusioned separate provinces one by one would seek entry into the United States. The ripe fruit would fall; there was little need to shake the branches prematurely.[3]

The government and public opinion of the United States were thus irritated when the new Dominion went confidently ahead to extend its boundaries to the Pacific and the Arctic, and to use its new strength to attempt to enforce its interpretations of the Convention of 1818 and keep American fishing vessels out of Canadian territorial waters except on the payment of licences which became yearly more costly. In his second annual message of 1870, President Grant referred somewhat waspishly to " . . . the colonial authority known as the Dominion of Canada, . . . this semi-independent but irresponsible agent [which] has exercised its delegated powers in an unfriendly way."

The Treaty of Washington ended the tension of the post-Civil War period in 1871. It removed the chief irritants in American-Canadian relations for the time being. It registered the tacit abstention of the United States from interfering with the united and separate existence of Canada. But it did not win for Canada cordial and understanding acceptance by the United States as a separate and evolving nationality in America. American opinion was profoundly unconvinced that Canadians either really desired to be a separate nation or in fact could become one.

The scepticism was natural and unavoidable. What Canada was, was unclear; it was covered by none of the definitions in the text books in the State Department. It corresponded to none of the experiences of the American people. More than that, Canada lacked the machinery for the direct negotiations with Washington by which its new status might have been made clear in practice to Washington. Washington was still bound by law and

3. As was frequently said in the contemporary American papers interested in annexation.

courtesy to deal with London. As a result, the continuing difficulties between the two countries were made even more irritating than they might have been. The renewed Canadian attempt to obtain a reciprocity treaty in 1874, rejected by the Senate, the reopening of the fisheries controversy in 1885, were all complicated by the need to obtain London's approval or to act through British officials. The prolonged depression after 1883 and the failure of Canada to attract immigrants to the prairie West seemed to justify American scepticism about the viability of the Canadian union, and to suggest that it would be wise to end the controversies and the Canadian need for reciprocity by a commercial union. That American continentalism in commercial form might lead on to political union also, some supporters of commercial union denied, others were content to leave to the working of time.

The proposal arose immediately out of business connections between the two countries. A Canadian capitalist resident in New York, Erasmus Wiman, who owned telegraph lines in Canada, and Samuel J. Ritchie, an American, the holder of an interest in the great ore body found in Sudbury, Ontario, first proposed the commercial union of the two countries in 1887. The Toronto *Globe* and the New York press took it up. The movement spread rapidly in Canada, and was supported by men like J. W. Longley, Attorney General of Nova Scotia and an avowed annexationist, and the English radical and historian, Goldwin Smith, an avowed continentalist. Then Sir Richard Cartwright, a descendant of an old loyalist family and a Tory turned free-trade Liberal, made it part of the program of the weakened and divided Liberal party. By 1890 it was renamed "unrestricted reciprocity" to meet Canadian objections to the political implications of commercial union and to avoid tariff difficulties with the United Kingdom.

So groomed, "unrestricted reciprocity" possessed great electoral appeal. Canada desperately needed markets. Agriculture and business were depressed; Canadian emigrants were flocking to the United States; Confederation and the National Policy had not yielded the fruits expected of them. The McKinley tariff threatened to complete the work of ruin. Then James G. Blaine, Secretary of State in the administration of President Benjamin Harrison, took a hand in what some Canadians suspected was a concerted game. Newfoundland had remained outside Confederation and needed entry for its fish to the American market even more than the Canadian Atlantic provinces did. In 1890 Blaine concluded a convention with the Newfoundland government known as the Bond-Blaine convention by which Newfoundland fish would enter the American market. The Canadian government saw this as an attempt to divide British America and lever the separate pieces into the American union. It succeeded in blocking ratification of the convention by the Imperial parliament. Blaine then privately invited the Canadian government to send delegates to Washington to discuss unofficially a treaty of reciprocity. The Canadian government, with mistrust but with no choice in face of the public desire for reciprocity and the Liberal program of unrestricted reciprocity, consented to do so. When the Canadian government had thus revealed its interest, indeed, its need, Blaine discussed the subject of the talks with the opposition journalist, Edward Farrer, once editor of the *Mail* and now of the *Globe* of Toronto and an avowed annexationist, who published the interview. While Blaine may have regarded this as an act of retaliation for a premature disclosure of the unofficial talks by the Canadian government, there can be no doubt that the manoeuvres of this bitterly anti-British and anti-Canadian politician from Maine were designed to weaken Canada and to assist the Liberals win the coming campaign for unrestricted reciprocity.[4]

To say that there was an international conspiracy to disrupt the Canadian union would be to strain the evidence at present available. If there was, it was defeated by the exposure of a

4. Accounts by leading authorities flatly differ in their interpretation of this passage; see C. C. Tansill, *Canadian American Relations, 1875–1903* (Toronto, 1943), pp. 424–80, and D. G. Creighton, *John A. Macdonald: The Old Chieftain* (Toronto, 1955), pp. 548–53.

pamphlet written by Farrer. A friendly printer gave incomplete galley proofs to members of the Conservative party. From these it was possible to see that Farrer was pointing out the many means by which the United States could put pressure on Canada, such as by denying Canadian fish entry to the American market and the withdrawal of bonding privileges, and make the continued existence of the country even more difficult than it was. The intent of the pamphlet was not of itself necessarily treasonous, but in an election year it was certainly possible to infer that it was. Prime Minister Macdonald read from the proofs at the opening meeting of the campaign in Toronto. His election manifesto followed: "A British subject I was born, a British subject I will die. With my latest effort, with my utmost breath, will I defy the 'veiled treason' that with sordid means and mercenary proffers would win our people from their allegiance." The cry won what D. G. Creighton has called the most important election in Canadian history, the National Policy was sustained, and a chastened Liberal party shed its policy of unrestricted reciprocity and its disloyal Canadians.

It was well that Canadians in the election of 1891 and its aftermath made their decisions to resist the commercial attractions of American continentalism. The next decade was to see the end of British power in North America. A token power only on the continent since the withdrawal of the garrisons in 1871, the possibility of its reassertion remained in the naval bases at Halifax and Esquimalt. By 1901 the founding of the modern American navy, the assertion of American hegemony in the Venezuelan crisis, the need the United Kingdom had for American friendship in the Boer War, and the price of that friendship in the unconditional abrogation of the Clayton-Bulwer Treaty which gave the United Kingdom equal rights with the United States in an Isthmian canal, all marked the ending of British power in America.

Masked though it was as the beginning of Anglo-American friendship, the change had profound and dangerous consequences for Canada. The great safeguard of the evolving colonial nation-hood was now ended. American dislike and scepticism of that anomalous contradiction of American experience and American continentalism might now have unchecked expression. Though it is seldom remembered even in Canada, the Venezuelan crisis aroused for the first time since the Civil War the possiblity of American invasion. As in 1812, there was American rejoicing at the prospect of an easy conquest; Canada, rather than Cuba, might have served as an outlet for the martial spirit of America. Unfortunately for such hopes, the Canadians were not fighting against the horrors of British rule, and not even the eager corre-spondents of William Randolph Hearst could have manufactured an atrocity north of the border which the most disingenuous reader would have believed. But the Canadian Ministry of Mili-tia had to prepare for mobilization, and only the British accept-ance of the American demand for a boundary commission averted trouble of the most serious kind.[5]

With the need to put relations with America in order, caused as in 1866–71 by Britain's isolation before an unfriendly Europe, recourse was once more had to the traditional device of a Joint Commission. The British half was now preponderantly Canadian in membership. The atmosphere was good. Secretary of State John Hay was genuinely desirous of good relations with the British Empire, and the British need to end all friction was clearly understood on all sides. The Canadians early recognized that a reciprocity treaty was out of the question, and all outstand-ing matters were then settled except that of the Alaska boundary. That finally had to be passed back to the normal processes of diplomacy, that is to say, to the disposition of power politics.

In the Alaska boundary controversy Canada was to learn a sharp lesson in the disadvantages of being a small nation in a world regulated by power politics. It was also to learn the cost of being the residuary legatee of a declining empire. From the Anglo-Russian treaty of 1825 Canada had acquired with British

5. G. F. G. Stanley, *Canada's Soldiers* (Toronto, 1960), pp. 273–75.

Columbia in 1871 a boundary with Alaska defined in the treaty but not demarcated on the ground. Despite the publication of Russian and American maps showing the Alaskan panhandle as an unbroken band of land separating British territory from the sea at any point, some Canadians began early to believe that the boundary gave them access to the sea at one or more points. The only official attempt to put this view on record was, however, mismanaged by the British minister at Washington in 1889, that Sir Lionel Sackville-West better remembered for his ineptitude in another matter. Thus Canada had left the American claims practically unchallenged until the Yukon gold rush of 1897 made it a matter of great moment to have the boundary settled and demarcated. The matter so far was only a comment on how rash a thing it is to attempt to govern half a continent on a shoestring; something is bound to be left undone.

The Canadian government was never in any doubt as to the comparative weakness of its claim to access to tidewater. But it thought there was a case a lawyer might argue and it did hope that if a case were argued, a compromise settlement might be reached. There were in fact the elements of a bargain after 1899 in the American desire to end the Clayton-Bulwer Treaty by trading the abrogation of that treaty for Canadian access to one of the inlets that penetrated the panhandle. Had it not been for the Boer War, the United Kingdom might have been able to win some such concession in return for giving up its rights in an Isthmian canal. But the war so strengthened the American position that there was no need to make concessions. Moreover, the determination of Seattle and the state of Washington to keep the monopoly they had over the trade with the Yukon from competition from Vancouver made any unconditional concession by Hay impossible.

Thus the Canadians had committed themselves to claims meant as a basis for compromise when all ground for compromise was suddenly cut from under their feet by the abrogation of the Clayton-Bulwer Treaty. But any retreat would have aroused public opinion in Canada, which was already anticipating that once more, as Canadian tradition taught, the Americans would outsmart or outbluff the British and Canada would pay the forfeit.[6] At the same time the temper of the American government became both hard and truculent with the assumption of the presidency by Theodore Roosevelt. Roosevelt and his imperialist friends saw that there was no need for concession in view of the strength of the American case and the weakness of the British position. The Canadians he viewed as "bumptious provincials"[7] who in attempting a horse trade had ludicrously overreached themselves. He proposed to teach them a lesson. He sent troops to Alaska; he threatened to run the line unilaterally. Finally, he was persuaded to accept a joint commission "of impartial jurists of repute" as a way of letting the obstinate Canadians down as lightly as possible. Even this Roosevelt made a farce by appointing three gentlemen of repute indeed, but none of whom was impartial. The chastisement of Canada ended in bitter recrimination when the unfortunate British member of the other half of the commission, Chief Justice Alverstone, caught between the bland inflexibility of the American and the angry intransigence of the Canadian members, did manage to arrange a compromise, not judicial but diplomatic, in a secondary issue of the dispute.

The Alaska boundary award was a humiliating experience for Canada. Canadians felt they had been treated with contempt by the American government and let down by the British. Much of the resentment was directed, interestingly enough, against the British who had tried their best to get Canada gracefully out of an impossible position, rather than against the Americans who after 1901 had showed little of the magnanimity which might have graced a position of such legal and diplomatic strength. But the lesson, a dual lesson as Canadians saw it, was learned. Hence-

6. F. W. Gibson, "The Alaska Boundary Dispute," *Report of the Canadian Historical Association,* 1945, pp. 25–41.

7. The phrase was Lodge's in a private letter: Howard K. Beale, *Theodore Roosevelt and America's Rise to World Power* (Baltimore, 1956), p. 128.

forth Canada must handle its own external affairs, neither relying on British support nor ever being caught in a direct trial of strength with the United States. American hegemony was henceforth not to be disputed as a fact of life in America, and Canadians felt that they must learn to live with that fact in their own way and, as far as possible, on their terms. For the future, in principle if not yet in form, Canada was on its own. Just as it had to find ways to avoid being drawn into commitments to the British Empire, so it must now devise ways to minimize American pressures. The solution to both problems seemed to be to grow in national autonomy.

Fortunately, plenty of time was allowed. In America the truculent imperialism of 1898 passed like a hot fit. Relations between Canada and the United States eased under the handling of James Bryce and Elihu Root. In 1909 the long-vexed fisheries issue was settled in Canada's favour by the Hague Tribunal largely upholding its definition of the Convention of 1818. The same year saw the Boundary Waters Commission established to handle the growing number of issues arising from the use of international waters for power or irrigation. The joint commission, so freely used in the past, had for Canada the great benefit of putting the two countries on the basis of legal equality. In order to be prepared for the time when all Canadian diplomatic business would be handled by Canadians, the Department of External Affairs was established in 1909 also. How small a department it was, and how important its business might be, is revealed in the fact that until 1946 the Prime Minister himself was Minister of External Affairs. The external affairs of Canada might at any time be the most important concern of its government.

The quiet which had fallen on American-Canadian relations was suddenly and violently shattered in 1911. Late in 1910 the administration of President William Howard Taft, disturbed by mounting criticism of the Payne-Aldrich tariff as a cause of the mounting cost of living, offered the Laurier government an agreement for reciprocal free trade on an extensive list of commodities.

After so many years of refusal, the United States had offered reciprocity. The Canadian government, under heavy pressure from the farmers to lower the tariff, quickly concurred. It seemed that, old and harassed as it was, it had won a new lease of life by offering the Canadian people what they had consistently and generally wanted since 1866, reciprocity with the United States. The Government was exultant, the Opposition depressed.

Then criticism began to be heard. The Opposition began to oppose the details of the agreement. The criticism grew in volume. Then the President and leading American politicians began to make public statements freely implying that reciprocity was only the first stage in the absorption of Canada into the United States. The criticism became a storm. The Government in haste went to the country in a general election and was defeated. For this defeat there were some solid and practical reasons. Canada's National Policy of tariff protection and railway building had brought into being a national economy. The industrialists, the business interests, the railways, and the railway workers were opposed to the admission of American goods and the sale of raw materials only for manufacture in the United States. But the main cause of the defeat of the Government, together with its losses in Quebec because of the Naval Service Act, was the anti-American sentiment of Canadians still sore from the humiliation of the Alaska boundary award. The anti-Americanism always latent in Canada exploded at the threat of a benevolent continentalism, perhaps more freely than it would have done before a more aggressive approach. "No Truck or Trade with the Yankees" was an emotionally satisfying slogan in which to indulge when the Yankees were obviously anxious to trade.

The outburst, hysterical in its extremes, at least was beneficial in that it discharged the suppressed resentments of a generation and perhaps drove home to thoughtful Americans that Canadians did intend what they said when they talked of being a nation. Certainly the relations between the two countries were to be more direct, tolerant, and mature after 1911.

For some time after 1911 Canadians had little thought to give to American relations, and fortunately there was comparatively little need. War in Europe was becoming increasingly more likely. In 1912 in the greatest secrecy the plans for the dispatch of a Canadian expedition to Europe began to be made by Canadian Military Headquarters. When war broke out, Canadian belligerency and American neutrality gave rise to no difficulty between the governments of the two countries. Yet Canadians, convinced that they were fighting for the freedom of small nations and for liberal principles of government against Prussian militarism, felt that American neutrality signified a reproach or a want of sympathy. Accordingly, they rejoiced at America's entry to the war; it meant not only help but also moral vindication. It must be said, for it was for a generation a sore point in Canadian sentiment, that the pleasure of the association in a common cause was soon marred. It was good to know that the Yanks had come after so long, but it was hard to be told that they had won the war. There was no Second Ypres, no Somme, no Vimy, no Passchendaele, among American battle honours. Canadians killed in battle and died of wounds numbered forty-eight thousand, Americans fifty thousand. Rudyard Kipling made the point for Canadians when he wrote:

> At the eleventh hour he came
> But his wages were the same
> As ours, who all day long had trod
> The wine-press of the Wrath of God.

All this might have been forgotten earlier than it was, had the magnificent leadership America gave the Allied cause in the last years of the war been followed by American membership in the League of Nations. That many Canadians, moved by what instinct it would be hazardous to say, profoundly desired. They were grievously disappointed when at last ratification failed to obtain the necessary majority in the Senate. That being the Canadian desire, it was ironical that membership of the Dominions in the League should have been one of the objections used to secure the defeat of ratification. While Canada itself in fact practised isolation within the League, liberal Canadians never ceased to lament America's absence from its membership. For all their insistent nationalism, most Canadians were eager to see America assume that leadership in the world to which they were convinced it was called. For, while no one stated the matter definitely, it was as obvious as gravity that Canada was moving out of the orbit of the British Empire into that of the United States. Canada, however, wished no more to be a satellite of America than a dependency of Britain. The new limitations and the old on Canadian nationhood would both be reduced to a minimum in common membership in the League. And as Canada above all needed peace to continue its evolution towards a stronger national unity, which the war had seriously impaired, and towards a greater economic development, which the war had indeed accelerated but at a grave cost in social tensions, in a League under American leadership lay the best hope of peace.

That hope was disappointed. Nevertheless, the years after 1920 saw the final acceptance, not only by the League but also by the United States, of Canada as a separate and for all practical purposes an international sovereignty. The United States government agreed to accept a Canadian minister in 1920, and only Canadian opposition, stirred up by concern over the rapid development of Canada's external relations, prevented appointment at that time. In 1923 the Canadian government first negotiated and signed a treaty with the United States by the instrumentality of its own agents alone, the Halibut Treaty. And in 1927 Mr. Vincent Massey was welcomed at Washington as His Majesty's Minister on behalf of Canada. The process of acceptance had been as slow, obscure, and indefinite as the evolution of the national identity of Canada itself.

The Period of Acceptance, 1927–1941

With American acceptance of Canadian nationhood began what may by anticipation be called the era of the "good neighbour" between Canada and the United States. This concept had been used by a Canadian of American-Canadian relations eighty years before President Franklin D. Roosevelt gave it currency. But the reality had at last arrived and Canadians welcomed it. Americans did also, even if their benevolence scarcely veiled a puzzlement, the shadow of the still-lingering scepticism of earlier days. It took a while for official Americans to learn to be at ease with Canadians in their new role as nationals. It was as though the former provincials were a parody, somehow vaguely irrelevant, of the Americans themselves. The wry similarity often led ordinary Americans to commit the unpardonable offence of declaring Canadians to be just like themselves. It was kindly, it was complimentary, and it was mistaken.

In the period of acceptance, however, Canadians were more at fault than Americans. It was the age in which many Canadians discovered that Canada was in America. It was useful information but exaggerated inferences were drawn from the simple geographical fact. For the great Winnipeg journalist, John W. Dafoe, to lecture on *Canada: An American Nation,* before Columbia University was a necessary piece of contemporary comment. Canada had become an American nation and it was important for Americans and Canadians to know how and why. But the busy tribe of historians carried the matter to great lengths. Professor Chester Martin found the roots of Canadian freedom, by no means wholly erroneously, in the colonial history of America. The frontier suddenly appeared in Canadian historiography, although the Turnerian frontier in fact and function was notoriously lacking in Canadian history. The American frontier was a transient experience; the Canadian frontier is perpetual. A great monument of scholarship, the Canadian-American Relations series, was reared to American continentalism, and was only saved from a complete overemphasis on the continental ties by the insistence of the Canadian scholars, A. L. Burt, D. G. Creighton, and J. B. Brebner, that the British connection had been midwife to Canadian nationhood. And the public orations on the undefended border waxed to a platitudinous climax, in bland ignorance of the fact that the British taxpayer had fortified that border and that the Canadian militia had been all but readied to defend it as late as 1895.

Exaggerated and often fatuous as the continental mood was, it was at least some degree better than frank hostility and open bickering. And it may have helped to explain why the most shattering of all depressions, unlike those of the nineteenth century, did no damage to American-Canadian relations. No dispute arose. Washington disliked the renewal in the Ottawa Agreements of 1932 of imperial preference for the first time since 1846, but more as a retrograde step in economic policy than as an injury to American interests. And Canadians in those days, untouched by the political and economic considerations patent to Americans, were stirred and encouraged by the leadership of President Roosevelt in the bitter days of the depression. His mild mixture of liberal socialism was probably more acceptable north of the border than south, for Canadians had begun to create the welfare state in some of the provinces at least. So infectious did the New Deal become, indeed, that the Conservative Prime Minister, Mr. R. B. Bennett, a millionaire corporation lawyer, produced a New Deal of his own in what proved to be a deathbed gesture, as the Canadian electorate turned it down to bring back Mr. Mackenzie King. And Mr. King at once used his new lease of power and the predilections of Mr. Cordell Hull to conclude the Trade Agreement of 1936—in effect, a reciprocity treaty—which has lasted from that day to this.

The common Americanism of those days was accompanied in Canada by an isolation almost as profound as that of the United States. Canada continued to be a member of the League. But the Canadian government knew that without the United States the League was helpless against Japan or Germany. Canadian opinion was isolationist, not in the American sense that America was sufficient to itself, but for Canadian reasons. French Canada feared another war would mean conscription, English Canada that it would strain national unity and again involve the nation to no purpose in another European blood bath. When the Canadian representative at Geneva had moved to strengthen the economic sanctions against Italy in 1935, he had been promptly repudiated by his government. Prime Minister King was no less definite in making it clear that Canada would consult its own interest first and those of collective security later. And Canadians rejoiced at President Roosevelt's promise of American protection in his Kingston speech of 1938.

Much of this isolationist sentiment after 1936 was owing to the growing realization that war was probably inevitable. The Canadian defence estimates, like those of the United States, began to mount. But Canadians were revolted at the thought of involvement in another war. It seemed, said the Prime Minister, "a nightmare and sheer madness" that "every twenty years" Canada should fight a war in Europe.[8] War, it seemed, could serve no conceivable Canadian interest; could then Canada be neutral? This debate went on as Canadians watched in fascinated horror the destruction of Czechoslovakia. Illogically, Canadian liberals denounced appeasement, not realizing that to do so was to condemn the same spirit of isolation that ruled in the United States and which most Canadians had seen their country practise with approval since 1920.

Canadian isolation, however, had no century of separation of mind and mood behind it, as had American. It was a new and not a characteristic attitude, one born of the period of American acceptance. Canadian sentiment, even to a degree in French Canada, still moved with British sentiment, not with American. As the British passed from appeasement to war, Canada passed from isolation to war. The mood of the country was horrified, tranced, fatalistic. Never was war declared with greater heaviness of spirit, but it was declared by an all but unanimous vote of Parliament. Only five members voted against the resolution, of whom

8. Canada, *House of Commons Debates*, 1939, II, p. 2419.

one was the universally respected Socialist leader, J. S. Woodsworth, a life-long pacifist.

Canada was once more at war while the United States was neutral. There was, however, no restraint and no friction. It is scarcely possible to doubt that the documents will reveal that the Canadian government knew the mind of the Roosevelt administration on the event and had no doubt of its sympathy. For there was no cold neutrality of thought and word in the United States, but all the help a merely formal neutrality could afford. And as between 1914 and 1917 but in greater numbers, Americans came north to volunteer for service in the Canadian forces. But when France went down in June, 1940, and the British Commonwealth faced Germany alone, two facts emerged. Only with the full aid of American industry could German-dominated Europe be contained, only with American help could Germany be defeated. Canadians waited anxiously for the American decision. The shock of the Anglo-French defeat meant that the power and position in the world which Britain had held had passed to the United States. If disaster followed disaster, the United States and Canada might stand alone between their oceans. The situation was registered by the bases-for-destroyers deal which gave the American Navy the bases it desired, including one in Newfoundland, for the defence of America. It was also registered in the establishment between the United States and Canada of the Permanent Joint Defence Board, also for the defence of America. Thus when Pearl Harbor came it was a disaster which, while it fell on the United States, was felt in Canada to be a common disaster. Canada had become what it had never been before, and had become permanently, an ally of the United States.

Canada and the United States as Allies, 1941–1945

The American declaration of war on Japan and on Germany and Italy had as one of its first consequences for Canada the entry of American armed forces into Canada. The reason was to expedite communication by land and air to Alaska and Russia and by air to Europe. At the same time the American Navy and Air Force began construction of their bases in Newfoundland, not at that time part of Canada, but strategically of first importance to Canada. The Americans came to the Canadian Northwest as allies, but their manner was often that of occupying forces. The American temper after Pearl Harbor was understandably one of urgency. But in the American forces, both in command and in the ranks, Canadians once more encountered the old impatience with Canada's separate existence and the deficiencies of a provincial and relatively poor society, and the old inablity to treat Canadian nationhood with respect. More serious was the question of Canadian sovereignty. It suffered serious infringement; American forces in Canada operated under American command and under American law.[9] The Canadian government had to agree in the interest of the common cause, to this invasion of its undoubted right to have friendly forces subject to Canadian law, as were the British, French, Poles, and other members of national forces training in Canada. The result was the revival in Canada of the old image of the domineering, headstrong, and tactless American.

In the European theatre no such problem arose. The Canadian insistence on Canadian command of Canadian forces sometimes seemed tiresome to the British and absurd to Americans. But it was generally satisfactorily settled, being indeed part of the larger question of Anglo-American command. Canadians fought under British and American command in Italy; the Canadian Army fought on the left in the invasion of Europe, and even had the American 101st Infantry Division under command in the fall of 1944. The First Special Service Force was a wholly joint formation of Americans and Canadians picked for special combat tasks and mingled without regard to nationality.

In the Pacific not even the question of command arose. It did,

9. The whole subject is dealt with in Stanley W. Dziuban's *Military Relations between the United States and Canada, 1939–1945* (Washington, 1959).

but in a very different context, for Australia and New Zealand, who rightly saw the Americans as saviours which Canadians never did. Canada, apart from the defence of Hong Kong, took little part in the Pacific war. After the end of hostilities in Europe a token contribution of a brigade, to serve under American command after American training, was made, but the war ended before it saw service.

During the war Canada supported the organization of the United Nations, despite reservations on the part of Prime Minister King, as an organization to make and police the peace. In the United Nations as a wartime alliance Canada, though it had no part in shaping the strategy of the war, did have a place of unusual importance in matters of supply, a result of its extraordinary industrial development during the war. It was also a result of the extent of the Canadian war effort. The nation of some 12,000,000 people had, without compulsory service except for home defence until 1944, 1,000,000 men and women in its armed forces. Besides financing this military effort and the development of war industry, it gave some $4,000,000,000 to its allies other than the United States, together with an interest-free loan of $100,000,000 to the United Kingdom. It received not one dollar in free aid from anyone,[10] despite statements to the contrary by two presidents of the United States, and countless other Americans with less obligation to be correctly informed.

Canadians had entered the war in heaviness of spirit. They fought it grimly and won little national distinction. Its battle memories are of the squandered heroism of Dieppe, the obscure gallantry of the fighting on the east coast of Italy, the failure to close the Falaise gap, the bloody clearing of the Scheldt and Maas deltas in the early winter of 1944. The First World War had brought Canada membership in the company of nations, the Second only a sense of duty done in common. Victory held no

10. Canada did receive seven of the over-age destroyers in the destroyers-for-bases transaction and was of course enormously aided indirectly by being given access to American industrial resources and American advice.

prizes, and peace revealed a world dominated by the good neighbour, who was also the American colossus.

The main objects of Canadian policy after 1945 were therefore to preserve Canadian sovereignty and to avoid being isolated with the United States in America. The historic dependence of Canada upon its European connections was now transmuted into the basic principle of Canadian foreign policy, that independence in America is a function of Canada's ties with the rest of the world.

The formation of the United Nations in 1945 was an opportunity to realize that principle by joining a world organization for collective action in preventing war and through the social and economic agencies attempting to do something to overcome the disparities of development and welfare among the nations of the world. The lingering doubts of Prime Minister King with respect to binding commitments were overcome by Mr. Louis St. Laurent and Mr. Lester Pearson, and Canada began to play an active role as a "middle power" in the United Nations. Canadians were sincere in their hope that the United Nations might prove itself an effective organization and there has been none of the North American isolation in its conduct as a member of the United Nations that characterized its membership in the League of Nations.

None the less, as the League had been the means by which Canada entered the community of nations, so the United Nations has been a means whereby Canada might pursue an independent course in world affairs. That that course has been independent when independence mattered, the record of Canada in the United Nations reveals.

When it became apparent that the chief hope of the western powers, the Security Council, could not function in face of the Soviet vetoes, Canada sought an alternative in the North Atlantic Treaty Organization. In many ways NATO particularly suited Canadian needs. It balanced the United States with western Europe. It brought together in one system the two poles of Canadian external policy, the United Kingdom and the United States. It seemed to embody the "North Atlantic triangle" of which Canada was the third angle. So greatly did Canada desire to win European confidence in NATO that it made the serious decision to place a major part of its armed forces at the service of NATO in Europe rather than in its own empty and now strategically important North, although without altering its own defence structure.

For the sake of the common defence of the NATO alliance, then, Canada after 1949 sacrificed its concern with its own sovereignty in America to its desire for the success of NATO in Europe. The decision was right in every respect, but it did underline the new problem of how to avoid impairment of sovereignty in the defence system of North America. A joint declaration of February, 1947, proclaimed that the defence of the continent would be planned by free discussion among equals, and implied that no American bases would be established on Canadian territory.[11] Then the Visiting Forces (United States of America) Act passed in June, 1947, brought all personnel of allied troops stationed in Canada under Canadian law. But when Newfoundland entered Confederation in 1949, the operation of the declaration and the Act was blocked by the American rights in the air and naval bases leased in 1941. The Permanent Joint Defence Board did make recommendations which brought the rights of American forces into line with those stationed elsewhere in Canada, but the bases were maintained. The Newfoundlanders were pleased, for obvious reasons, but informed Canadians felt that the situation in Newfoundland should have been brought into line with the declaration of 1947. Their fears were underlined when in 1952 Canada "under persuasion" granted a twenty-year lease of an air base at Goose Bay in Labrador.[12] With those exceptions,

11. R. A. Spencer, *Canada in World Affairs, 1946–1949* (Toronto, 1959), p. 287 and pp. 306–13.

12. B. S. Keirstead, *Canada in World Affairs, 1951–1953* (Toronto, 1956), p. 175.

the co-operation begun for the air defence of North America went forward on a much more tolerable basis than the wartime collaboration. The American operation of the Pine Tree line caused no difficulty; that of the DEW line led to criticism in the Canadian press, but this arose out of a misunderstanding of the necessities of travel in the Arctic. The organization and command of NORAD in 1958 conferred the position of second-in-command on a Canadian officer. So tremendous an integration of defence forces, with the awful implications of the decision its commanders may have to take, has proceeded, it would seem, harmoniously. The basic difficulty arising from joint command was not the question of sovereignty, or of possible clashes of national interest; it was that of the disproportion of the two allies. The full implications of the adjective "permanent" in the title of the Permanent Joint Defence Board, the existence of which had been reviewed and confirmed in 1947, had been brought home to Canada. The defence alliance with the United States was not one from which Canada could withdraw if it would,[13] and to the extent of the alliance its independence was qualified.

The Years of Friction, 1952-19——

It would not be fitting here to recount the grievances against America which Canadians had accumulated since 1941, and

13. A policy of neutrality is, in the author's opinion, quite impossible for Canada in all matters pertaining to the defence of North America, which means, of course, the defence of western Europe also. If Canada did not co-operate in this, the United States would obviously have to take such measures as it thought necessary. Moreover, Canadian interest and the genuine wish to be a loyal, if not an uncritical, ally of a kindred people rule out neutrality.

On the other hand, an alliance for North American defence does not commit Canada to approval or support of such things as the over-extension of American power in Taiwan and Okinawa, or of the sometimes brash methods used in balancing the military threat of Soviet power. Neither does it require nuclear armaments for Canadian forces; a highly mobile "conventional" army would seem to meet the military needs and circumstances of Canada best.

Cf. James F. Minifie, *Canada: Peacemaker or Powder Monkey* (Toronto, 1960), a plea for Canadian neutrality.

which they began to express with mounting vehemence after 1952. The extent and nature of those grievances have been set out with admirable fairness and a pleasant, discriminating touch by two American observers, Joseph Barber and Miriam Chapin.[14] While none of them is unimportant and while in some of them much justice lies on the Canadian side, there is not one of them which could not be dealt with by firm and proper Canadian action. It is obvious, for example, that American investment in Canada must be governed by Canadian law and that it is not likely to find more attractive fields elsewhere in the world. Nor does it greatly matter that Americans and Canadians share the same popular culture; after reading the same comic strips, and the same periodicals, Canadians remain as distinct as they ever were. What differentiates the two people are things far deeper than the mass culture of North America which both countries share and both created.

One thing, however, does lie between America and Canada which must be noted because of its sombre and fundamental character. That is the death of Herbert Norman, Canadian Ambassador to Egypt. The relations of Canada with the United States were gravely and permanently impaired by the investigation, or naming, of Canadian civil servants by the Senate Internal Security Subcommittee. Nothing revealed more clearly to Canadians how intimate the relations of the two countries had become, for the material relating to Mr. Norman had been supplied by the government of Canada in a routine and confidential exchange of information. The establishment of the loyalty of its servants is surely one of the most sovereign of the acts of government. The only objective conclusion Canadians can draw from the Norman case is that nothing, not even the honour of a friendly neighbour, is exempt from the exigencies of American politics, and that the government of Canada must govern itself accordingly.

14. Barber, *Good Fences Make Good Neighbors;* Miriam Chapin, *Contemporary Canada* (New York, 1959).

How extensive Canadian grievances were, and how deep re-sentment ran was revealed in the political upheaval of 1957. The elections of 1957 and 1958 were like that of 1911, long-delayed explosions of long-accumulated resentment against the United States. Everything from the Arctic bases and the Trans-Canada Pipeline to the Suez crisis was taken as proof of negligence by the Liberal government in protecting Canadian interests. The charge was of course unjust, but in the heat of the erupting re-sentment, Canadians were more concerned to lash out at the United States than to judge the Liberals impartially. The two elections and particularly the spectacular Conservative sweep of 1958 were not of course to be interpreted as merely anti-Amer-ican explosions. The most important thing about that of 1958 was that it meant that Canadians had at last recovered from the trauma of the fatal conscription election of 1917. But anti-Amer-ican sentiment was strong and general.

It must be recognized that the nature of the relations between Canada and the United States is such that explosions of Cana-dian resentment will occur periodically. The intimacy of the re-lations of the two people and the disparity of power between the two states make it inevitable that American indifference and power will provoke Canadian resentment from time to time. The United States, it is to be hoped, will remove such grievances as can be removed and will suffer the outbursts philosophically, as befits a great power. Canada, it is to be hoped, will avert the accumulation of grievances by dealing firmly and responsibly with grievances as they arise, and so keep the explosions at as long intervals as possible.

Canadian Nationhood and American World Power

The main treatment, then, for Canadian resentment at actions or attitudes of the United States is for the Canadian government to deal with the causes of resentment as Canadian responsibilities that can in most instances be dealt with in and on Canadian terms, and when necessary at Canadian cost.[15] Canadian nationhood is one of the firmer facts of twentieth-century life. It is a fact fully and cordially recognized and accepted by the American government and people. Canada is free, within the limits of world power politics, to continue to work out its own destiny.

What then is that destiny? Canadian destiny is an evolution in progress. It has not been defined. It cannot yet be defined. But certain elements may be perceived. It is part of Canada's destiny to be an independent nation in America. Canadian nationhood consists of a political nationality resting on two cultures, one Franco-Catholic, one Anglo-American. There are other diversities also, but none not subsumed in the political nationality. The national life of Canada rests on a northern economy, the exploitation of the resources of a country largely arctic or subarctic in climate. The political life of Canada is that of a monarchical and parliamentary democracy, in which the popular will of the electorate is realized by the legal sovereignty of the Crown in Council and the Crown in Parliament. The independence of Canada has been realized in free association with the other members of the Commonwealth. That association is of inestimable value to Canada, not only because it nourishes in Canada the institutional heritage of the Commonwealth, but also because it is an antidote to the isolation and continentalism that Canada's American character and affinities breed. Finally, since dependence and association have always been elements of Canadian destiny, Canada now stands at the beginning

15. Such devices as the Joint Committee on Trade and Economic Matters, set up in 1953, may be helpful, but given the basic American attitude towards Canada, are only too likely to become endeavours to "explain" American policies and attitudes to Canada. Canadian policies and interests are far more likely to be understood and appreciated by the experts of the Department of State than by members of the Cabinet or the Congress. (The Hays-Coffin unofficial committee of 1957–58, and its two reports are exceptions to this observation.) In short, American-Canadian "understanding" is a matter for experts. An understanding in popular terms is almost impossible because, paradoxically, the two peoples superficially understand one another too well.

of a significant experiment in reconciling the substance of political independence with the need imposed by the power politics of the nuclear age for limitation of national sovereignty, if like-purposed powers are indeed to be able to act for the common defence.

If then Canada's destiny is in its own hands, why is it disturbed by fear and resentment of America? The answer is plain. What Canada really fears is not the old America, but America in its new role of world power. It fears that America in seeking to maintain its world power will make demand after demand on Canada, each reasonable in itself, until the substance of independence is modified out of existence. More than that, it fears that the United States, in some sudden convulsion of the world balance, will simply occupy Canada. Circumstances may easily arise in which the United States would have no more choice than Canada. It fears also, out of its knowledge of the American temperament in action, that such an occupation could be made needlessly, or that once made, would not be unmade. For, the government and people of the United States, while they have come to accept Canadian nationhood, do not understand it and therefore do not value it. Canadian concern with this fact arises from a mature awareness that while Americans in their friendly way accept Canada as a neighbour, they are not in their heart of hearts convinced that Canadian nationhood is possessed of a moral significance comparable with that of their own great nation.

If a great simplification may be attempted, in order to cut to the root of the matter, this is so because Americans, by being Americans, are in a measure precluded from understanding Canada. Americans are a people of the covenant, as Clinton Rossiter has so brilliantly demonstrated. That may be taken to mean three things. The first is a need for a measure of uniformity; the covenant is among the like-minded. The second is that the covenant to a degree cuts the covenanted off from the uncovenanted. Third, the covenant implies not only uniformity and isolation, but also a mission. America is a messianic country periodically inspired to carry the republic into other lands for the liberation of the Gentiles, the lesser breeds without the covenant.

Nor is this the whole of the fundamental character of America. If the mission is denied, as by present-day China, if the messianic complex is thwarted, then occurs that search for the domestic traitor, the uncovenanted, which today is called McCarthyism, from which America has suffered so much, and from which Canada too suffered in the death of Herbert Norman.

This fundamental American character, a barrier to understanding any nation, is particularly an obstacle to understanding Canada, for Canada is not the creation of a covenant, or a social compact embodied in a Declaration of Independence and written constitution. It is the product of treaty and statute, the dry legal instruments of the diplomat and the legislator. It is the pragmatic achievement of the little-regarded labours of clerks in the Colonial Office and obscure provincial politicians, still unknown to the world. Beneath their work the moral core of Canadian nationhood is found in the fact that Canada is a monarchy and in the nature of monarchical allegiance. As America is united at bottom by the covenant, Canada is united at the top by allegiance. Because Canada is a nation founded on allegiance and not on compact, there is no process in becoming Canadian akin to conversion, there is no pressure for uniformity, there is no Canadian way of life. Any one, French, Irish, Ukrainian or Eskimo, can be a subject of the Queen and a citizen of Canada without in any way changing or ceasing to be himself. This is a truth so fundamental that it is little realized and many, if not most, Canadians would deny its truth, but it is central to any explanation or understanding of Canadian nationhood.

Canadians might deny its truth, as Americans would, because they tend to have, as part of the mass culture of America, a stereotype of monarchy in mind as arbitrary government. But the English monarchy, and indeed the French, was a free monarchy. The king's task was to uphold the law, not to make law, still less to govern by personal will as an autocrat. British monarchy in Canadian history has been doubly freedom-giving in its action, both in the evolution of parliamentary and responsible government, and in the function of the Crown as the symbol of national integrity. To be a British subject never meant subjection in Canada; Canadian government has never been arbitrary, but always lawful in character. And to civil and political freedom Canadians chose to add social equality. Neither rank nor privilege survived in Canada, monarchical though the government was.

It is also because Canada is not founded on a compact that the final governing force in Canada is tradition and convention. Self-government came to Canada by administrative change gradually worked out rather than by the proclamation of principles. No one could say what the goal of self-government was, for it was evolving pragmatically. For long no one could declare what Canadian destiny was to be, and when Macdonald did speak of "the great and powerful nation" in North America, the designation he used for it was out of the past, the title of the Kingdom of Canada. It was the Burkean partnership of the generations to which Canadians aspired. For if among the spiritual forefathers of America were John Calvin, Robert Browne, and John Locke, those of Canada were Bishop Bossuet, Edmund Burke, and Jeremy Bentham. The moral significance of Canadian nationhood then is like to America's, that it is the expression of a free society, but, Canadians would claim, whereas American society rests on assent constantly renewed, Canadian society depends from the historical and objective reality of law personified by the monarch and modified as need arises by the Crown in Parliament.

Because Canada arrived at freedom through evolution in allegiance and not by revolutionary compact, it had not a mission to perform but a destiny to work out. That destiny has never been manifest, but always exceedingly obscure. It could not be defined, for by definition it was self-defining. But it has proved to be a destiny to create on the harsh northern half of a continent a new nation, sprung from the ancient traditions of France, nourished in British freedom, and, it must be gladly said, fortified by American example. It is a nation which has sought not a separate and equal existence, but an equal existence in free association, and that principle of free and equal association it would wish to govern its relations with the world power of America. Its moral quality lies in the fact that it is a free society; its moral significance may lie in that, in a world where absolute sovereignty is more than ever a fiction of the text books, Canadian nationhood has at least put the proposition that association and equality are not incompatible terms, that nations may in free association, by careful definition and great patience, make mutual accommodations of sovereignty without loss of independence.

Chapter iv

The Relevance of Canadian History[1]

The Characteristics of Canadian History

Relevance, for the purpose of this chapter, may be understood to mean the relations between the history of Canada and the histories of other communities. It also means the orientation given to Canadian history by the interaction of those relations with the environment and historical development of Canada. How those relations and that orientation are defined will in turn suggest the interpretation of Canadian history embodied in a work approaching completion. Relevance, finally, means what universal or philosophic significance belongs to the Canadian historical experience.

By Canadian history also is to be understood one history, not one French and one British, but the entire history of all Canada.

1. Presidential address read before the Canadian Historical Association, Queen's University, Kingston, Ontario, June 11, 1960.

There are not two histories, but one history, as there are not two Canadas, or any greater number, but one only. Nor are there two ways of life,[2] but one common response to land and history expressed in many strong variants of the one, it is true, but still one in central substance. The reason for this is that the history of Canada after 1760 is only a continuation and extension of the history of Canada before 1760. There is but one narrative line in Canadian history.

The argument of this chapter is equally simple. It is that the relevance of Canadian history takes its rise in the relations and orientations which result from four permanent factors in that history. These are a northern character, a historical dependence, a monarchical government, and a committed national destiny, committed, that is, to special relations with other states.

The Factor of Northern Orientation

The northern character springs not only from geographical location, but from ancient origins in the northern and maritime frontier of Europe. That frontier extends from Norway by Scotland and the North Atlantic islands to Greenland and Canada. Within that area from mediaeval to modern times there is discernible a frontier of European culture developing across the northern latitudes in which the forward movement was largely by sea. It was not a Turnerian frontier, but it was a frontier in every sense, and it was this frontier which began the exploitation and settlement of Canada. Many of its characteristics survive in Canada to this day, and presumably will continue to do so indefinitely.

The historical characteristics of this northern and maritime frontier are clear and definite. The most evident was that of coastal and riverine settlement. The largely Precambrian geology of the region afforded few extensive or fertile plains. The shelves in the fjords, the estuaries of seasonal rivers, the terraces around

2. A. R. M. Lower, "Two Ways of Life: the Primary Antithesis of Canadian Life," *Report of the Canadian Historical Association, 1943.*

bays, these were the foothold and the baseland the northern frontier afforded to settlement. Even the Laurentian trench in America simply raised the foothold to continental proportions but did not change its character. Moreover, the maritime character of the frontier tended to settlement by the sea, even when extension of the economy inland was possible.

The settlements sometimes consisted of small port towns, but the characteristic mode was the family farmstead. This was the centre of a complex of arable land, pasture, fuel land, and hunting ground much more delicate in its relationships than those of a farmstead in a more favourable climate and a more fertile soil. Land near the stead yielded vegetable and cereal foods, if climate permitted. The outfields and hill pastures gave pasture and hay. The adjoining forests or bogs furnished firewood or peat. The summer was a season of sowing, herding, and gathering in, the winter a season of concentration in house and byre, of relaxation or rationing according to the summer's yield.

The winter was also the season of hunting, whether for food or fur. The northern frontiersman in this lull penetrated the wilderness and used it to supplement the returns of the farmstead. The dependence of any one farmstead or settlement on the hunt varied from place to place, but hunting as a seasonal occupation was always one characteristic of the northern frontier.

Fishing was equally a supplementary occupation to a degree also varying with locality. It too furnished an addition to the diet, and even forage for the cattle. The run of the fish in the rivers was seasonal, and curing by smoking or drying made fish, for example the eel fishery of the St. Lawrence, an indispensable part of the diet of the northerner. The sea fisheries were summer fisheries, but tended to equal cattle raising in importance, to take the men away for the season and thus to demand co-operative effort and specialization. They might also yield a staple for trade.

The fisheries, it may be supposed, were the origin of the seafaring that made possible both the migration of the frontier across the North Atlantic and also the amount of trading which took place between it and the central lands of the European metropolis. Certain it is that the northern frontier was much more a maritime than a land frontier, a character which to a curious degree Canada retains even yet, and which will increase again as arctic navigation develops. The pioneers of that frontier were not long hunters or the *voortrekkers,* but fishermen seeking new fishing grounds, seamen-farmers in quest of new island pastures, Viking voyagers who sought in new lands whatever fell to them of plunder, trade, or homestead.[3]

The northern and maritime frontier had its own northern economy with characteristics equally explicit. It was an extensive and a gathering economy, dependent on new lands, new seaways, and the transport the seas and rivers afforded. It required a base of arable soil and habitable climate for the farmstead settlements. The farmstead was a highly self-subsistent unit, but it was the base of an economy which as a whole was an exchange economy to a high degree. The surplus staples of fish, fur, and timber, with exotics like arctic ivory and oil, falcons, and Polar bears, earned the funds with which to buy the metals, the cereals, the church goods, and the luxuries the northern settlements needed or desired. Some of the traffic was interregional; it was, for example, its timber that made Vinland of primary interest to the Greenlanders.

That the Canadian economy historically has been an economy of this kind requires no demonstration. The great staple trades have been extensive, in-gathering trades. The population which carried them on lived in and worked from relatively narrow bases of good land in the sea inlets and river valleys; most of Canada is simply a hinterland extensively exploited from the soil base of the St. Lawrence and Saskatchewan valleys, and from the delta of the Fraser. The Canadian economy has also largely bought its external supplies by the sale of surplus staples.

The first discovery and early exploration of the lands which were finally to be united in Canada were the outcome of the ad-

3. A. W. Brøgger, *Norse Emigrants* (Oxford, 1929).

vance westward of the northern and maritime frontier of Europe and the extension of the northern economy to America. These discoveries and the first occupation of Canadian shores were made by way of the northern approach. Somehow, by methods yet only guessed at, the Viking frontiersmen, the Bristol traders, and Norman fishermen made their way across the North Atlantic. Their sea skill and navigational science were so far developed that they could use the brief and uncertain easterlies of late spring and early summer which blow as the belt of the westerlies shifts north with summer to make their way across by a northern route.[4] They did not, like the Spaniards and the Elizabethan English, use the long but certain southern route of the trade winds. The discovery and occupation of Canada was separate and distinct from the discovery and occupation of the Americas.

Nor was it the result of high-pitched, scientific exploration aimed at the trade of Asia. It was the outcome of the piecemeal ventures of Norse seamen-farmers probing the northern seas for new harbours and fisheries, new hay meadows and timber stands. The process is scantily documented. Government archives record it scarely at all; it can now be understood and comprehended only by an understanding of the character of the northern frontier and economy, an understanding which is as bold an extension of the hints of the sagas as were the original voyages themselves.

The evidence, however, is slowly accumulating to suggest that between the last connections with Greenland and the voyages of the Bristol seamen there was no break in sea knowledge or experience.[5] The Bristol men, with the knowledge of the Azoreans and, presumably, of the Normans and Bretons, were taking over the western half of the old Norse sea empire, and were being caught in the westward tug of the northern frontier. It is scarely to be doubted that their own efforts would have discovered the Newfoundland fisheries if John Cabot and Henry VII had not im-

4. D. W. Waters, *The Art of Navigation in England in Elizabethan and Early Stuart Times* (London, 1958), p. 577.

5. Vilhjalmur Stefansson, *North West to Fortune* (New York, 1958).

posed on their limited and practical efforts the scientific concepts of the Italian navigators and the first imperial impulse of Tudor England. In any event, the outcome was the same. Asia was not discovered, nor was the English empire founded in the fifteenth century, but the Newfoundland fishery of the English west country, and of Normandy and Brittany, was in being by the opening of the sixteenth.

This, then, is the first orientation of Canadian historiography. Canadian history is not a parody of American, as Canada is not a second-rate United States, still less a United States that failed. Canadian history is rather an important chapter in a distinct and even an unique human endeavour, the civilization of the northern and arctic lands. From its deepest origins and remotest beginnings, Canadian history has been separate and distinct in America. The existence of large areas of common experience and territorial overlap no one would deny. History is neither neat nor categorical; it defines by what is central, not by what is peripheral. And because of this separate origin in the northern frontier, economy, and approach, Canadian life to this day is marked by a northern quality, the strong seasonal rhythm which still governs even academic sessions; the wilderness venture now sublimated for most of us to the summer holiday or the autumn shoot; the greatest of joys, the return from the lonely savagery of the wilderness to the peace of the home; the puritanical restraint which masks the psychological tensions set up by the contrast of wilderness roughness and home discipline. The line which marks off the frontier from the farmstead, the wilderness from the baseland, the hinterland from the metropolis, runs through every Canadian psyche.

The Factors of Dependence: the Economic

We come now to the second factor, that of dependence, of the external ties and background of Canadian history. Canada throughout its history has in varying degrees been dependent economically, strategically, and politically. The northern economy, for example, was self-subsistent only at the base. Even there it was not necessarily so, as the extinction of the Greenland colonies grimly demonstrated, and as the plight of the prairie provinces in the 1930's re-emphasized. As a whole, however, the northern economy was a highly dependent one. It was a hinterland economy dependent on the sale of a few basic staples and a few exotics in a metropolitan market.

That is, the whole culture of the northern and maritime frontier, to succeed as well as survive, required from outside a high religion, a great literature, and the best available science and technology to overcome its inherent limitations. These very limitations of climate and of material and human resources made the frontier dependent on a metropolitan culture for those essentials. The alternatives were extinction or complete adaptation to the lowest level of survival in northern conditions. Was not the basic difference between the north European and the Eskimo that the former had a central and metropolitan economy and culture on which to draw, while the latter had none until very recent times and lived in a wholly and wonderfully self-subsistent culture?[6]

The northern economy, then, was a dependent one, both for the markets which absorbed its staples and exotics, and for the supply of the needs of mind and body which raised life on the northern frontier above the level of subsistence and enabled it to produce in Iceland the literature of the sagas and in modern Canada the political fabric which unites the technology of a highly civilized and industrialized baseland with the exploitation of the resources of a harsh and enormous hinterland.

6. And is not the extraordinary readiness with which the Eskimo adopts the techniques and implements of modern culture an indication of how necessary such a metropolitan culture is for a life of more than survival in arctic conditions? Surely contemporary anthropology has no more fascinating study than that of the fusion of the Eskimo culture with that of the Canadian frontier which is proceeding in the far north today. One may hope that Canada is at least giving those wonderful people the central base they lacked for so many unrecorded centuries.

The Factors of Dependence: the Strategic

If the northern and maritime frontier has been economically dependent, it has been even more so strategically. Down to the fifteenth century it was defended more by remoteness and poverty than power. Its own population and resources were too slight for the task of defence. The decline of Danish sea power and the rise of the Hanseatic League left it entirely defence- less, as the English raids on Iceland in the fifteenth century revealed. And with the development of the ocean-going sail- ing ship in the same century, the northern frontier became ex- plicitly dependent on sea power. "Empire of the North Atlantic" would be naval empire.

It was not, however, until the end of the seventeenth century, when the use of naval power became systematic after the Dutch conquest of the Spanish power at sea and the balance of power in Europe was extended to include the Americas, that the north- ern frontier in its Canadian extension actually came into the stra- tegic pattern of European empire. The capture of Port Royal in 1710 and the Hill-Walker expedition against Quebec in 1711, though a failure, may be taken as marking the beginning of the operation of European strategy through sea power upon the northern frontier.

The result was, because French sea power had declined rela- tively to the British since 1692, that New France had to develop a holding policy and count on victory in Europe to regulate the Euro-American balance. This policy succeeded until the Anglo- American conquest of Canada in 1760. Canada then became wholly dependent on British sea power, if indeed one may refer to Canada when for the first and only time the northern frontier was politically united with the developing agricultural and industrial power to the south. That transient union was, however, to be bro- ken in part by the Quebec Act, in part by the American War of Independence. The Anglo-American empire had failed to ab- sorb the northern frontier with its primitive economy and Indian tribes, and the break-up of the empire in America was preliminary to the larger disruption caused by American independence. The sea power of Britain was then the decisive factor in the survival of Canada, but it did not operate alone. Conscious and deliberate choice by Canadians and Nova Scotians made their survival a complex historical process by which the northern community resumed its identity in the North Atlantic system.

The situation after 1783 of course remained fluid and uncertain. Canada and the maritime colonies remained part of the northern economy and strategically dependent on Britain. The new balance achieved in 1814, as described in Chapter One, was registered in the boundary convention of 1818 and completed by the Oregon Treaty. These diplomatic achievements and their military backing revealed how firmly a part of British policy was the defence of Canada and the retention of a strategic check on the United States. Until the rise of the iron warship, the timber of the northern frontier, whether in the Baltic or on the St. John and the St. Lawrence, was a necessary element in British sea power. But after the emergence of the United States from the Civil War as a great military power and the gradual British withdrawal from the Americas, Canadian military strength by no means rose in correspondence with the decline of British power. Canada, in fact, as Laurier remarked to Lord Dundonald in 1902, was henceforth defended by the Monroe Doctrine.[7] Canadian dependence had taken a new, an American, form.

The dependence was by no means complete, nor was it ever to prevent Canada as a member of the Empire from making war abroad. The situation did, however, make it clear that the resources of the northern economy had proved insufficient to create a military power of significant stature except in alliance with one or other of the great powers. What had been accomplished, however, had been the transformation of dependence into free association and free alliance by the development of national self-government in the Empire and America.

7. G. F. G. Stanley, *Canada's Soldiers* (Toronto, 1960), p. 294.

The Factors of Dependence: the Political

The factors of economic and strategic dependence were until the end of the nineteenth century also expressed in terms of political dependence. The French exploitation of the fisheries and the fur trade, with the zeal of French missionaries and an intermittent interest in a trade route to the Far East, had led to the development of the French empire in America. On the private commerce of the fishery and the fur trade, with their need of defence and regulation, the French Crown imposed its own interests in the conversion of the native people and the colonization of Acadia and Canada. Underlying these interests was the strategic purpose of establishing in New France a base for commerce with the new lands and, if possible, with the Far East.

This partnership of royal power with the northern economy was often an uneasy and a fretful one, as when the *coureurs de bois* after 1672 defied the royal policy of limiting the fur trade and carried their enterprise westward. Yet in the end the two were reconciled in the imperial purpose after 1700, when France began to use its northern base and its continental spread to confine the English colonies to the seaboard.[8] The primitive northern economy had penetrated the continent by the great river systems, as the Swedish Vikings had Russia, and the rivers, the canoes, the fur traders, and the Indians were the means used to check the advance of the English settlers. The union of the primitive and the sophisticated, of war and trade, of small means and ranging enterprise which characterized the northern culture, was never better exemplified than in Canadian captains like Iberville, or in the French empire in America in the eighteenth century.

The first British Empire had developed similar characteristics in the north. The Hudson's Bay Company was the outcome, and

8. How serious this purpose was is revealed by the annual payments made by the French Crown for the government and defence of New France from 1661 to 1760.

a continuation of, the search for the Northwest Passage. It too needed metropolitan protection, and only escaped absorption into the French empire by Marlborough's victories in Europe. On the New York frontier in the days of William Johnson the English developed the same alliance with the Indian and the northern economy of the fur trade that the French had done. And in Nova Scotia the same factors of colonial dependence and imperial purpose produced Halifax. When the British empire in America broke up in the War of Independence, it was in part because the differences between the old northern empire of France and the old colonies of England had not been reconciled. And when the disruption was complete, the union of northern dependence with imperial strategy ensured that Nova Scotia and Canada, the northern elements of the fishery and the fur trade should remain within the British Empire.

British America had the same northern character as French America, a base for the fisheries and the fur trade, for trade by the St. Lawrence with the continental interior, and for naval power and Northwest exploration. How true this was is apparent if a glance is taken at what Imperial policy actually did in British North America between 1783 and 1871. It not only paid much of the cost of government and defence; it preserved the territorial claims to which the Dominion was to be heir. From 1818 to 1854 it employed Franklin and his fellow explorers in the same scientific exploration that under Cook's genius had led to the opening of the Pacific and the colonization of Australia and New Zealand. At the same time it halted Russia in Alaska by diplomacy, and forestalled it in the arctic archipelago[9] by the great feats of naval exploration of Ross, Parry, and M'Clintock. By so doing, it laid the groundwork for the Canadian occupation and development of the Arctic. This Imperial policy was not only a major element in Confederation, in ensuring its achievement, but also in delivering to it, as to a new metropolitan base, the whole of

9. L. P. Kirwan, A *History of Polar Exploration* (New York 1959), pp. 77–78.

northwestern and arctic hinterland. By this stroke, the northern and maritime frontier of the empire of the North Atlantic became a northern and a continental one in the Dominion of Canada.

The new Dominion was meant to be a new nation. Yet its northern character, the limitation imposed by its situation and climate meant that in fact the new nation was to remain still dependent on other states, the United Kingdom and the United States, for capital, technology, and defence. The continued support of the United Kingdom was needed to discourage the intermittent continental stirrings of the United States. American engineers were needed to build Canadian railways, and British capital to finance them. Anything like instant and full-blown independence was neither possible nor desirable. The two factors of national aspiration and external support were slowly reconciled by the gradual transformation of continued dependence in a free association which ensured the needed support while affording the desired independence. The character of Canada's association with both the Commonwealth and the United States is thus the outcome of its historical development as a northern frontier.

The Factor of Monarchical Institutions

That association derives also from another aspect of the northern frontier, the form of its political dependence. Although its remoteness and the separation of communities created a spirit of local independence, the limitations of its economy made for political dependence. That dependence found the most ready historical and the most satisfying psychological expression in allegiance to a monarchy. Until the rise of modern communication it was difficult to maintain unity in states based on popular sovereignty. Moreover, in Canada two historic factors combined to make monarchical allegiance a particularly satisfying political tie.

One was the French monarchical tradition of the old regime. The royal government of France, and particularly in New France, was largely military in organization and combined much personal independence in its subjects with a regular hierarchy of rank and subordination. It was also paternalistic in that all ranks looked to the higher for the defence of rights and the grant of help. The exercise of the power conferred on the king and his officers by the system was extraordinarily humane, and the bureaucracy remained a surprisingly serviceable one, partly because the personal royal will might always be invoked to correct hardship or bestow favour, partly because it was suffused with the religious principle that royal authority was a trust to be exercised for the doing of justice and the granting of mercy. The failure of the early British regime to capture and perpetuate some of this spirit is to be explained not so much by the fact of conquest as by the pressure of the "old subjects" and loyalists for government favours and by the fears aroused by the French Revolution. None the less, much of the old attitude to government and public service survived in French Canada.

The second factor was the great strengthening in the bond of allegiance in British America caused by the American Revolution. The decisive act of the Revolution was of course the throwing off of allegiance by the Declaration of Independence. Equally decisive was the resolution of the loyalists to maintain their allegiance. How clearly the matter was understood is shown by the declaration required of settlers in British America after 1783, in which they were required to acknowledge "the Authority of the King in his Parliament as the Supreme Legislature of this Province."[10] Not only allegiance was required, that is, but an acknowledgement of that theoretically unqualified supremacy of the Crown in Parliament against which the thirteen colonies had revolted. The second British Empire was founded explicitly on allegiance and the legislative supremacy of the King in Parliament.[11]

In the British American colonies after 1783, however, an es-

10. A. G. Doughty and D. A. McArthur, *Documents Relating to the Constitutional History of Canada, 1791–1818* (Ottawa, 1914), p. 22, Instructions to Dorchester, Sept. 16, 1791, No. 35.
11. Except in the matter of taxation.

sentially democratic or popular spirit, fed by the practices of the Protestant churches and by local needs, operated to turn the constitutional development of the colonies away from the monarchical ideal affirmed after the Revolution towards popular and American practices. The local democracies from time to time and in varying degrees used the assemblies to express and assert interests in conflicts with Imperial policies or the outlook of the colonial administrations. The assemblies made the Speaker their leader, and sometimes, especially in Lower Canada, a tribune of the people and the leader of a popular opposition. By the use of committees and commissioners to administer expenditures of money voted by the legislature, they assumed executive powers and of course strengthened their own hands by the distribution of patronage. The recurrent clashes which led up to the rebellions of 1837 in the Canadas were thus not only political struggles between the assemblies and the entrenched councillors and governors; they were a constitutional conflict between an ideal of government essentially republican and one essentially monarchical.

The former was the "elective system" of Papineau and the republic of Mackenzie, the latter was the "responsible government" of W. W. Baldwin and Etienne Parent. The effect of the latter, the application of the concept of ministerial responsibility to a colonial constitution, was quite clear. It was the preservation of a British, hereditary, and monarchical executive acting on the advice of local ministers. By the application, the democracy of the colonies was reconciled with the allegiance of the colonists. Political sovereignty in Canada could become democratic, as democratic as in a republic, while legal sovereignty remained unaffected and not less powerful in its ancient form, the monarchy. British America might walk in its own political paths, but never lose contact with its constitutional heritage of political and civil liberty upheld by law declared in the Queen's courts and made by the Queen in Parliament.

While responsible government was a Canadian concept amplified by Joseph Howe and sanctioned by Durham, there can be little doubt that in Canada the compromise its adoption embodied was made possible in large and perhaps decisive measure by the great British migration that began after Waterloo and was at flood tide when responsible government finally became a basic convention of Canadian government at mid-century. English Canada had until 1812 become largely American in population and in the functioning of its institutions. After 1815 the old American stock, both loyalist refugee and mere immigrant, was swamped by the new British immigrants. Political power in the English Canada was taken from the native-born by the British-born by the eighteen fifties, a process which happened, to a less degree and much more slowly, in the Atlantic provinces. The names tell the story, Baldwin, Hincks, Gowan, Draper, Harrison, Macdonald Brown—all were British born.[12] Only the French remained to represent the native-born in the first exercise of the new powers of self-government.[13]

It is also to be noted that while the governors ceased to be active executives with the adoption of the principles and practices of cabinet government, and became in theory constitutional or limited monarchs, they by the change also became the guardians of the conventions of responsible government.[14] These indeed had, if not to be evolved, as they were still evolving in the United Kingdom, at least to be adapted to Canadian conditions. The governors became, from the glimpses our present knowledge affords us, the mentors of politicians who themselves had to learn the manifold and often subtle applications of the conventions. In turn, because the succession of governors was periodic and on

12. J. M. S. Careless "Mid-Victorian Liberalism in Canadian Newspapers, 1850–67," *Canadian Historical Review*, Sept., 1950.

13. This of course partly explains why self-government was used in Canada to reform the institutions of English Canada and to confirm those of French, with the one great exception of the abolition of seigneurial tenure.

14. W. M. Whitelaw, "Responsible Government and the Irresponsible Governor," *Canadian Historical Review*, Dec., 1932, pp. 364–86, reveals how freely the governors exercised their power after 1848.

the average much more frequent than the succession of hereditary monarchs, no doubt the experienced politicians and permanent clerks often became the instructors of the governor. The immediate point is, however, that all these men were of British birth before Confederation, with the single exception of Sir Fenwick Williams. None of them had parliamentary experience approaching that of Sydenham, but only two, Williams and Sir Charles Hastings Doyle, were soldiers, and all came from the British governing class and knew the traditions and nuances of parliamentary government and no doubt, even before Bagehot, had a very clear idea of the limitations which hedged a constitutional monarch.

Certain it is that by Confederation in Canada and Nova Scotia the politicians who achieved cabinet rank from time to time had learned and were at home in the mixture of traditional form and business-like dispatch with which the prerogatives of monarchy were exercised in the service of democracy. It was this familiar and valued working system that British American politicians thought infinitely preferable to the democratic presidency and the government of separated powers of the United States. The belief was not a mere provincial prejudice, but the sober judgement of mature and experienced men who had learned their art in one of the most difficult of all schools, a democracy of diverse ethnic groups. For it is to be remembered that there were not only French and English in British America; there were Highland Scots, Catholic Irish, and Lunenburg and loyalist Germans, all of whom had had small experience of parliamentary government, though as quick as the French to learn all the tricks of the game. In such a society responsible government had been made to work so that local communities and special interests could get done what they wanted done, if it were not blatantly contrary to the public interest.

Extraordinarily little republican sentiment, always to a degree endemic in Canada as in the United Kingdom, seems, moreover, to have survived in the last years of the generation after the rebellions. There was therefore a great consensus of opinion in both French and English British America that in any future union the basic institution of responsible cabinet government in the Queen's name should be embodied in the new general government and continued in the continuing local ones. "The Executive Government and authority of and over Canada continues and is vested in the Queen," was to be the most significant, as it is the most simple and direct of all the sections of the British North America Act. On that basic principle there was neither hesitation nor complexity to blur the simple, positive affirmation. The language is lucid, the intent unquestionable. Canada was to continue a constitutional monarchy.[15]

So insistent is the emphasis on monarchy in the Confederation debates and in the speeches made throughout the provinces that it is necessary to ask just what was meant by it. No one spelled it out. By inference from the whole of what was said and from the historical context in which it was said, it is legitimate to suppose that it meant on one hand the retention of personal allegiance to the Crown with responsible and parliamentary government, and on the other the avoidance of popular sovereignty (or democracy) and a federal union.

The desire to continue personal allegiance to the Crown, after liberal principles had triumphed in British America with the grant of responsible government, and at a time when British America was about by uniting to take a great and conscious step towards nationhood, calls for explanation. Responsible government, of course, had been a compromise in which parliamentary democracy had been combined with constitutional monarchy on the British model. The monarchical element was in fact central to the compromise. By it a number of things were accomplished, over and above the essential matter of maintaining the personal

15. I trust it is unnecessary to point out that in speaking of monarchy in this context I have in mind only a set of constitutional principles, and neither a sentimental royalism nor the regrettable Edwardian pomp which alienated the affections of so many Canadians from the outward expression of what is the core of the Canadian political tradition.

bond of allegiance between the Queen and her subjects in British America. One was the maintenance of the Imperial connection. The material bonds of empire, it is true, had ended with the commercial revolution of 1846–49. There was, moreover, no good reason, commercial or financial, still less military, why the connection between the United Kingdom and the colonies should be kept up. And there were those who looked to a speedy end of the connection. But there were other reasons, important to British America, for maintaining the tie. The main and central one was that the Imperial connection sustained the whole constitutional heritage of the colonies. Without the connection, the allegiance to the Crown would have ended and the monarchical principle would have been lost. With it would have gone the compromise of responsible government and all the gains made since 1837. The ending of the connection would have thrown the control of events into the hands of the extremists, *les rouges*, the Clear Grits, and, so do extremes meet, the old Compact Tories, none of whom valued responsible government, and all of whom would have plumped for republican institutions and annexation.[16]

With parliamentary and cabinet government would have gone other matters of value to the moderates and conservatives of that day, a few of which are still of value to most Canadians. One was the limited franchise and the idea that the franchise was a trust. Another was the British system of justice, challenged at the time of course by the principle of election applied to the selection of judges by the Jacksonian democrats across the border. Yet another was the sense of public rank and personal honour, then still strong in British as in French Canada. Finally, there was the instinctive feeling, an articulate perception in French Canada, that monarchical allegiance allowed a diversity of customs and rights under law in a way that the rational scheme and abstract principles of republican democracy did not. The monarchy, in short, subsumed a heterogeneous and conservative

16. As some of all of the three groups did in the crisis of 1849.

society governed in freedom under law, law upheld by monarchy, where the republic would have levelled the diversities and made uniform the various groups by breaking them down into individuals, free indeed, but bound by social conformity and regimented by an inherent social intolerance.

Such a levelling and uniformity was the work of the principle of popular sovereignty, of French Jacobins and American Jacksonians. The diffusion of power among the people gave rise inevitably to the demand that it be diffused equally, and Canadian radicals used the Benthamite formula of one man, one vote. The demand for representation by population was of course another application of the same ideal of political equality in a society of equals. What excesses that principle had led to in France and the United States all liberal and conservative Canadians at Confederation knew, and in their view Canada had been saved from it only by the repression of the rebellions of 1837. In a republic, it was felt, such a principle could lead only to anarchy or a Caesarian dictatorship, as it had done in France, as perhaps it had done in the United States at civil war under Lincoln. Again, the monarchy by ensuring that legal sovereignty rested on foundations independent of the results of the last election, ensured also, however political sovereignty might be diffused through the electorate, that the last essential of government, the maintenance of peace and order, would be independent of popular impulse.

Finally, the emphasis on monarchy by the Fathers of Confederation arose from their conviction that monarchical institutions had enabled them to avoid the necessity of resorting to a federal union in their scheme of union for British America. It was true that they had left the provincial governments in being. It was true that the scheme could be described and defended as a federal one. But they were persuaded that they had not recognized the principle of co-ordinate sovereignty, as they were convinced they had avoided those weaknesses of federal union which had plunged the United States into civil war. They thought in fact that, under the supremacy of the Imperial Crown in Parliament they had created a Canadian Crown in Parliament which would be actively supreme in the union as the Imperial power was supreme, if with a supremacy mostly latent, in the Empire. The union, to their minds, was a legislative union, not a federal or a quasi-federal one, and the anomalies of the special rights of French Canada, or provincial legislatures which possessed all the potent apparatus of responsible government, were no more striking than the many which the Empire in the amplitude of its constitutional variety had nourished from the covenant of Plymouth Colony to the latest experiment in Western Australia.[17]

The Factor of Commitment

The monarchical emphasis of the Confederation debates was unusual in Canadian politics, a response both to the profounder than usual reflections of the nature of Canadian government prompted by the work on constitution making, and also to the collapse of the American scheme of government in the Civil War. But as a consequence, the monarchy continued in its central place in the Canadian political tradition to become after 1931 the symbol of association with the Commonwealth, and that association is one part of the commitment of Canada. The second part is the new and unfamiliar alliance with the United States. The association with the Commonwealth expresses exactly the Canadian desire for an association compatible with independence. The alliance with the United States, however, raises the question of whether an alliance between states so unequal in power and so intimately linked by economy, language, and culture, can in fact be compatible with independence. The question has already been discussed in the foregoing chapters. That the American alliance is a major and a growing commitment of Canada has already been emphasized in the preceding chapter. The point made here is

17. I am indebted to Mr. Peter B. Waite, "Ideas and Politics in British North America, 1864–1866" (Unpublished Ph.D. Thesis, University of Toronto, 1953) for the substance of this paragraph.

that the preservation of Canadian integrity in that alliance will depend upon the relevance of Canadian history, on its cultural and moral significance in universal history, and on American recognition of that relevance.

The Maintenance of the Northern Nationality

The relevance of Canadian history lies, then, in the morally defensible character of Canadian purpose in maintaining a northern nation in independence and vigour in the circumstances of the second half of the twentieth century. The first element of that purpose is to be found in the realization of the northern economy. For that Canada possesses the necessary land bases in the great river valleys of the south. It possesses also in ever-increasing measure the industrial power by which to bring to bear on the Canadian Shield and the Arctic the technological skill and power to conquer the north. It possesses in its scientists and its universities the knowledge and the capabilities in research to fathom the deep secrets of the north and to measure the hair's-breadth difference between disaster and success in northern development.

In this, there need be no thought of turning the Canadian back on the south. The northern economy has never been self-sufficient, nor can it ever be. But it is manifest from Canadian history that every time that Canada has sought a destiny in the south, disaster has threatened. Every time that impulse came from outside, from the imperial aims of the House of Bourbon in 1701, from the European strategy of La Galissonnière in 1749, from the desire of Great Britain to tap the commerce of the Mississippi valley between 1783 and 1846. The effort was beyond the resources of a northern economy and a northern people, and every time Canada was thrown back upon the Shield and the Northwest.

That is not to say that ordinary, or even special, ties to southward need be harmful; on the contrary. Reciprocity, on Canadian terms, as in 1854 and 1936, strengthened the northern economy. The great areas of overlap in the Atlantic provinces, the Eastern townships, the Ontario peninsula, in Michigan, Wisconsin, Minnesota, and the prairies, and on the Gulf of Georgia, reveal how rough the division between the northern and the continental economies have been. But the division was made and remains, and the areas of overlap have been areas of exchange in which the two economies mingle and strengthen one another by a traffic in raw materials, goods, and skills which, however, is the exchange that arises from difference, not from uniformity.

The northern economy is a clear and evident thing, explicit in history. Not so definite, but still discernible, is what may be called the northern outlook of Canadian arts and letters. The mere reflection in art of northern scenery, or northern life, important though that is, is not what is meant. What is meant is the existence in Canadian art and literature of distinctive qualities engendered by the experience of northern life. These are a tendency to the heroic and the epic, to the art which deals with violence, a tendency not only realized in the work of E. J. Pratt, but also indicated in that of Louis Fréchette, and in the much less successful writings of Charles Heavysege and William Wilfred Campbell. The later canvases of Lawren Harris and those of Emily Carr have this same heroic quality stylized.

That is the art of the hinterland. The art of the baseland is the lyric of Archibald Lampman, of Octave Crémazie, and the landscape of Cornelius Krieghoff and W. J. Phillips. The great cities of the baselands have their sophisticated art, of course, and that eludes the generalization attempted here, as it should. The reference is only to what is characteristically Canadian, not to what is universal as well as Canadian.

To the heroic and the lyric, the satiric is to be added. For northern life is moral or puritanical, being so harsh that life can allow little laxity in convention. But the moral affords the substance and creates the disposition for satire. Canadian literature has been comparatively rich in satire, from the parody of Sam

Slick's Yankee sharpness by a Tory loyalist to the extravaganzas on small town life of Stephen Leacock, or prairie rural life of Paul Hiebert. For satire feeds upon the gap between profession and performance, and the puritan both displays the gap more and sees it in other men's performance more readily than those of less rigid standards. The excellence of Canadian political and social caricature stands on the same satiric footing. In all these qualities, Canadian literature has of course affinities with both Scottish and Icelandic literature. They give promise of a literature, and an art, as idiomatic as it is significant universally.

Finally, the northern quality of Canadian life is maintained by a factor of deliberate choice and natural selection. As the American frontier has always been open, absolutely or comparatively, to Canadians, Canadians have always been free to live as Canadians or to become Americans. Many who make the latter choice do it with reluctance, but the choice is nearly always made on the grounds of greater reward or wider opportunity. That is, they have rejected the harder life and smaller material rewards of Canada. The result is that Canadians to an extraordinary degree are Canadians by choice. In consequence, Canadians become generation by generation more and more a northern people, either because northern origins have fitted them for northern life, or because they have become adapted to it.[18]

The Character of Canadian Nationality

One element in that choice has often, perhaps usually, been the desire to maintain the Canadian allegiance. Here, perhaps, it will be permissible to elaborate something touched on in the preceding chapter. Canada has never been a country royalist in

18. Lest this seem harsh, as it is not meant to be, let a well-known Canadian-American speak: "So far as the Canadian academic migration is concerned, this means an awareness of the growth of a North American nationality in which the old loyalties are cherished, not for provincial exclusiveness but for the maintenance of the enduring verities which embody the ideals of human rights and freedom as expressed in the history and institutions of both Canada and the United States." James T. Shotwell, in *Canadian Historical Review*, Mar., 1947, pp. 42–43.

sentiment any more than Canadian society has remained formally hierarchical in structure. Canadian manners have always tended to be simple, and Canadian society has steadily become a society of social equals. But for many reasons it has been a monarchical country, and not a country of the social compact like its great neighbour. The reasons for this have been historic rather than sentimental. Allegiance means that the law and the state have an objective reality embodied in the succession of persons designated by Parliament and hereditary right. They do not rest on contemporary assent, although the policies and acts of government do. In Canada therefore government possesses an objective life of its own. It moves in all its parts at popular impulse, but if there were no impulse, it would still move. In the United States government is subjective. It is designed to move on popular impulse, and if there is no impulse, the movement soon flags and falters. The republican government, massive as are its institutions, historic as is its momentum, in a very real sense rests upon assent periodically renewed. Such a government requires as basis a society of great intrinsic unity and conformity in which a consensus works to a common end. In Canada, a country of economic hazard, external dependence, and plural culture, only the objective reality of a monarchy and the permanent force of monarchical institutions could form the centre and pivot of unity. Allegiance was a social and political necessity of national existence and prevailed over the manifest and insistent attraction of republican institutions and republican liberty.

Not life, liberty, and the pursuit of happiness, but peace, order, and good government are what the national government of Canada guarantees. Under these, it is assumed, life, liberty, and happiness may be achieved, but by each according to his taste. For the society of allegiance admits of a diversity the society of compact does not, and one of the blessings of Canadian life is that there is no Canadian way of life, much less two, but a unity under the Crown admitting of a thousand diversities.

For this reason it is not a matter of political concern that Canada has two major cultures and many smaller ones. It would be foolish to deny that the dual culture is one of history's many harsh gifts to Canada, that the duality arose from the ordeal of conquest and suppression and that it has given rise to friction and to weakness. But it is manifest that it is a gift which admits of transmutation into something rich and strange, into a political order as liberal as those which Lord Acton, by way of example, thought approached nearest the ideal.[19] The transmutation can be wrought when the two cultures are seen as variations on a common experience of the land and history of Canada, and of the common allegiance in law and spirit to the traditions and the Crown of that land.

That common experience has created a common psychology, the psychology of endurance and survival. Canadian experience teaches two clear lessons. One is that the only real victories are the victories over defeat. We have been beaten many times, defeat has been our national portion in America, but we survive and we go on in strength. And our experience teaches also that what is important is not to have triumphed, but to have endured. The pride of victory passes, but a people may survive and have its way if it abides by the traditions which have fostered its growth and clarified its purpose.

The common experience extends also to the Canadian achievement of the secret of Commonwealth, that free association in self-government is a bond of union which may yet outlast the controls and authority of empires, however strong. That achievement was the work of Canadians of both the major stocks, it is the

19. "If we take the establishment of liberty for the realization of moral duties to be the end of civil society, we must conclude that those states are substantially the most perfect which, like the British and Austrian empires, include various distinct nationalities without oppressing them."— *Home and Foreign Review*, II, 25, quoted in David Mathew, *Acton: the Formative Years* (London, 1946), p. 180. Acton's instances seem somewhat unfortunate now, but his point that the state ought not to be identified with society is more valid than ever as the instances of totalitarian regimes multiply.

outward expression of our domestic institutions, and its spirit informs Canadians of all other origins with an equal pride in free institutions elaborated by the Canadian political genius. We must bring to the working out of the American alliance the same persistence in freedom and the same stubborn ingenuity, recognizing always that this special relationship with the United States is different in kind from the historic associations of Canada and can in no sense take their place.

In the end, that common experience extends to a common affirmation of moral purpose, the purpose which makes Canadian history relevant to universal history. Canadians, if one may judge by their history, believe that society cannot live by the state alone. Society has its own autonomous life, which is sustained by sources which may enrich the life of the state, but over which the state has neither authority nor control. Those sources are religious or moral, and flow into society only through persons. The personality of the individual citizen, then, is the object of the justice the state exists to provide and of the welfare society exists to ensure. The individual thus possesses the ultimate autonomy, since he is the end to which both state and society are means. But that autonomy carries with it a sovereign obligation to respect and safeguard the autonomy of his fellows, primarily by manners, which are the dealings of man with man, and secondarily through the social and political order. So reciprocal and delicate a complex of justice, welfare, and good manners may function only in an organic unity of state, society, and individual. It was such a unity of king, church, and people Canadians, both French and English, inherited from their remoter past and have elaborated in their history as a monarchical and democratic nation.[20]

The preservation of such a national society is not the unique mission of Canada, but it is the central fact of Canadian his-

20. K. C. Wheare, *Modern Constitutions* (London, 1951), pp. 43–45; N. Mansergh, *Survey of British Commonwealth Affairs, 1939–1952* (London, 1958), pp. 369–75.

tory that it has been preserved and elaborated by Canadians in one of the largest, harshest, and most intimidating countries on earth. Canada, that is, has preserved and confirmed the essentials of the greatest of civilizations in the grimmest of environments. It is an accomplishment worthy of a better end than absorption in another and an alien society, however friendly and however strong in its own ideals. In that accomplishment and its continuance lies the relevance of Canadian history.

Chapter v

Canada under Stress in the Sixties: A Commentary

I

The decade which began in 1961 tested every assumption of the Canadian identity and tried every fibre of the national body. The stresses of the decade resulted from the tensions between the momentum of a hundred years of history and the drag of frictions counter to that history. The question at the end of the decade was, which would prevail, the thrust of national history or the brake of anti-national forces?

In retrospect, it is easy enough to record the causes of the change from the gathering momentum of 1961 to the faltering drive of 1971. At the end of a decade which may be termed revolutionary, the causes of the momentum slowing were clearly seen to be three. The first was the emergence of a new tone and temper in French Quebec, first the Quiet Revolution, then the drive of a growing minority to establish a French state independent of Confederation. The second, little noted but, it may be, not far short of the changes in Quebec in importance, was the relative decline of Great Britain in the world and the end of Britain as the exemplar and inspiration of Canadian life. The third was the realization of Canadians that American protection, investment, and friendship, long accepted as facts of Canadian life, would, if not restrained, carry with them the price, neither stated nor demanded but inevitable, of the complete Americanization of Canadian thought, government, and national purpose.

None of these factors was new, of course. French Quebec had never been completely happy in Confederation, and had never lacked those who questioned the benefits of Confederation for Quebec and sought to modify the terms of the original federation. When the decline of Britain began remains for the historians to decide. It perhaps first appeared with the Crimean War; certainly, many Canadians felt, it became evident with the First World War, with Gallipoli, Jutland, and the naval disarmament of the Treaty of Washington of 1921. To some Canadians, from 1775 on, the United States rather than Britain had seemed to offer a model for Canada to emulate, and after 1921 that admiration for American ways was underpinned by a need for American capital in a world in which financial supremacy had passed from Britain to America. Canada before 1914 throve on pounds loaned, after 1921 on dollars invested.

II

If these causes may in the light of history prove to be of much the same magnitude of importance, there can be no doubt that in the decade of 1961 to 1971 the emergence of the revolution in the tone and temper of Quebec was of much the greatest notoriety. The causes of that change may be found elsewhere.[1] What is pertinent here is to isolate the essential elements of the changes pro-

1. See, for example, Ramsay Cook, *Canada and the French-Canadian Question* (Toronto, 1966); Richard Jones, *Community in Crisis: French-Canadian Nationalism in Perspective* (Toronto, 1967).

ceeding in what was, before 1939 if not in 1960, one of the most conservative and even placid of Canadian provinces. It is of first importance to recognize that the change was revolutionary, at once a repudiation of the beliefs and institutions of the past, and a grasping for new beliefs and new institutions. The second element to be noted is that what was repudiated was almost wholly French, by origin or adoption. Quebec was really more in revolt against its own past than against Confederation.

In nothing was the truth of this more apparent than in the wholly secular and materialistic tone of the revolutionary demands. The Roman Catholic Church was, it is true, not attacked; much worse, it was ignored. To everything the revolutionaries sought the Church was irrelevant, no longer even a hindrance. No possible change in Quebec could have been more absolute, because Quebec society, in mind, aspiration, and behaviour, was almost wholly the creation of the Church. But in the years following 1900 the growth of modern industry and of Montreal had undone the work of two centuries of jealous, tender fosterage by the Church. The Church had become a private association, much as a church in Protestant society; Quebec had become a secular, materialistic state, neuter and amoral, much as if it were a Protestant country. This was the groundwork and the major fact of the revolution. The remainder was the working out of that parting from the intellectual and spiritual tutelage of the Church.

The third element essential to the revolution in Quebec was therefore the attempt to create a secular and materialistic society. To this there at least seemed to be few barriers. The French Canadian, poor or well off, accepted readily the models before him. One was that of the United States, near, fascinating, resplendent with efficiency, bright with speed, and uncompromised by any political tie, such as those that existed with Britain and the rest of Canada. Equally attractive, possibly in some ways more so, was the model of neighbouring Ontario, prosperous, growing, yet lazy with all those comforts of bourgeois life which were the aspirations of middle-class French Canadians and the better-off members of the trade unions. The spiritual influence of the Church, still strong, the older values of French Canadian culture, might continue to question the quality of the American or Ontarian ways of life, but to little effect. Revolutionary Quebec had opted to be North American, on whichever model—efficient, prosperous, worldly.

If this were all, then the revolution should have eased relations between Quebec and English Canada, and diminished the role of Quebec as one of the more obvious reasons for the independence of Canada from the United States. Certain things, however, in themselves also elements of the revolution, stood in the way. The first was *nationalisme*.

When the *nationalisme* of the Québecois began is still a matter of simple assertion by historians of one persuasion or another. To the *nationaliste* historian it was early, previous to 1760; to the less involved perhaps from 1806, perhaps from 1837. It might indeed be salutary to ask if to the ordinary French Canadian *nationalisme* was not a fiction of a *nationaliste* élite descending from Garneau to Groulx.

Even that élite, however, was to be taken seriously as an important part of Québecois society, a markedly élitist community. The *nationaliste* élite began, not with the Canadian clergy, whose vocation was assured, but with the lawyers, the journalists, the politicians, whose professional futures were uncertain. They it was therefore who encountered the necessity of seeking openings in the world of politics and business dominated by English Canadians, and the necessity of a command of English for success. They it was who felt the humiliation of rebuffs, who developed that sense of inferiority almost inevitable in minorities, and which is the tap root of *nationalisme*.

As such it was understandable and excusable. But in recent times the *nationaliste* chose to base his claim on language and on culture. To do so was to create an unbridgeable barrier between *nationalistes* and all other people whatever, a barrier as strong as race or colour, if less apparent. Culture could rarely be transmitted except by birth and early upbringing. The emphasis on culture acted as a barrier particularly to English Canadians, to whom, unless they were social scientists, "culture" tended to mean personal cultivation and refinement. *Nationalisme*, accordingly, could only operate to divide English Canadians from French, and to destroy the Canadian political nationality. As it developed, it sought ultimate expression for cultural nationalism in political *nationalisme* by the secession of Quebec from Canada.

Séparatisme was still at the end of the decade a matter of an élite, to some degree of an élite within the established élite. Some French Canadians, however, such as Pierre Elliott Trudeau, Prime Minister of Canada from 1968, had sought a new character for Quebec in an invigoration of the democratic forms of its political life. The great majority were content to let things take their course, or to profess some milder version of *nationalisme*, as expressed by the political party known as the Union Nationale. In Quebec, nevertheless, as an élitist society, the ideas of today's élite might well be the opinions of tomorrow's majority. There was grave danger that what élitists thought one day Québecois would think the next.

What all nationalists said was that the Québecois should be master of their own destiny—the old Quebec cry of *maîtres chez nous*. It was a fascinating example in the taxonomy of minority grievance. There was in fact not one evil suffered by the Québecois that was not the outcome of their own way of life freely chosen and deliberately pursued, with one major exception. That was the rocky and barren character of so much of the province of Quebec, like the corner of Labrador designated by Jacques Cartier as the land that God had given to Cain. Like New England or the Maritimes, it was a land that could only be abandoned by most of the people it produced, unless they willed to live in poverty. Yet the whole effort of the French Canadian clergy and nationalist writers, the great Archbishop A. A. Taché excepted, was to persuade French Canadians never to abandon the sacred soil of *la patrie*.

Not only was this unwise, leading to the deep poverty portrayed by Louis Hémon as patiently to be borne;[2] it also meant that the deep, the sorrowful, the abiding glacial poverty of Quebec was the work not of the English, but of Quebec itself and the clerico-nationalists who, as time was to show, had unwittingly misled and betrayed its people. Matters would have been much worse than they were had it not been for the English presence, with capital, commerce, and industry. But, of course—for such was the nature of the tribal passion of nationalism, such were the absurdities to which the hyperstatization of cultural differences lead—it was the English who were blamed by the clerico-nationalists for the ills and sufferings of Quebec. Nothing had happened in Quebec that would not have been alleviated, if not remedied, by such a movement of people out of Quebec to the prairies as had occurred in Ontario from 1860 to 1914. (True, they would have been lost to Quebec, as those who went to New England were,[3] but not to Canada, where their presence might have given the Canadian West a different character.) But Quebec had chosen, guided by its spiritual and intellectual leaders, to cling to the barren ribs of the Laurentians and the Shickshocks.

No English Canadian would be thanked for such harsh speaking, even were it accepted as true. It was, however, perhaps not a very important truth. What was more important, as responsibility always rests on the stronger, was to ask why the English did not carry the French with them in the making of the Canadian nation, that political nationality of diverse cultures. That they did not was as much or more a reproach to the English as the withdrawal into Quebec was to the French clerico-nationalists, and necessarily the greater one, as the English were the dominant group.

A nation, the Canadian historian Frank Underhill has finely said, consists of people who have done great things together. This, no-

2. In *Maria Chapdelaine* (Montreal, 1913).

3. Not, of course, the repatriated Jules-Paul Tardivel, the fervent nationalist writer.

toriously, the English and French had rarely done, or rarely on terms of proportionate equality. They were co-workers in the fur trade, but all the *engagés* were French and very few of the *bourgeois*. The opening of the West was more Cartier's work than Macdonald's, but the settlement of the West was largely left to English, American, and European immigrants. Only a few heroic clergy had settled the scattered islands of French on the prairies. Hardly any English Canadians had the wit to join Henri Bourassa in his early effort to create an all-Canadian sense of nationality. Relatively few French served in the two great wars that were the main enterprises of Canada in this century; those few—their roll of honour led by the splendid name of Vanier—had distinguished themselves, but they could not compensate for what had always been an unequal balance.

The imbalance, it is important to repeat, was more the doing of English than French Canadians. The English did not proceed by public repression or even as a rule by secret discrimination. No minority of different origin, except the Germans of Alsace, had been as well treated by a majority in law and politics as the French by the English. No English Canadian had any need to feel guilt with respect to the public treatment of the French of Quebec. The disproportionately large concessions made to them may be argued to have been a perennial drag on the growth of the Canadian nation. But in personal affairs the conduct of most English Canadians could only be condemned. They were guilty of the supreme human crime of indifference. What began in the 1840's as a considered policy of toleration became a practice of indifference, wounding indifference salved by occasional bouts of patronizing attention. It was this that had created the two solitudes.[4] It was not so much that the English failed to respect their French compatriots; it was rather that they failed to understand and cherish them. All people are open to warmth and consideration in others, none more so than French Canadians. But warmth and under-

4. Hugh MacLennan, *Two Solitudes* (Toronto, 1945).

standing consideration they rarely received from the federal government of Canada and from English Canadians, at least until the passage of the Official Languages Act in 1969.[5]

Both English and French Canadians, then, were to be indicted, one for a parochial and rather shabby nationalism, the other for a provincial obtuseness and personal coldness, both unworthy of a people raised in the Canadian heritage. To make such a double indictment, however, must inevitably be quite unhelpful unless the reason for it is made apparent. That reason lies in the faith, expressed however inadequately in this book, that Canadian nationality, combining in one citizenship and allegiance two national communities and a number of cultures, was in fact a human experiment of which the outcome was vital to Canadians of both languages and of some interest to humanity. For if the state can rest only on race and language, or the imperial control of weaker races by stronger, men must be seen to have abandoned the promise of the great religions, the possibilities of human reason, and all that has been called civilization.

The question before Canadians between 1961 and 1971 was, therefore, whether French Quebec was to establish a nation state, or whether the terms of the Canadian experiment could contain both its developing purpose of a multi-cultural community, and also the *épanouissement* (the efflorescence) of spirit and ambition in French Canada. This, if not easy, was not impossible. The real drift of the Quebec revolution was for French Canada to enter the main stream of North American life without losing its French identity. It was as certain as anything human that its best hope, if not its only hope, of doing so lay in the continuation of the Canadian nationality as conceived in 1867. In other terms, the Canadian nation would continue by the cordial acceptance, on the part of all Canadians, of the cultural nationality of French Canada—not of Quebec alone—and by providing example, aid, and sympathy for

5. This Act made English and French equally official languages throughout all Canada, with language districts for minorities of either language. *Statutes of Canada*, 17–18 Eliz., c. 54.

the reform and invigoration of the economy of Quebec and, one might add, of New Brunswick. The former was the purpose of the Royal Commission on Bi-lingualism and Bi-culturalism which reported in 1965 and 1967, and the latter the policy of the federal government of Lester Pearson from 1963 to 1968. Linguistic and cultural equality and economic aid, it was hoped, would diminish the discontents which gave rise to *nationalisme.* This was quite possible, with cool statesmanship in Quebec. Ontario Hydro had preceded Hydro Québec by over fifty years; the powers of a Canadian province were sufficient to create at least a semi-socialist economy, probably the only kind which would overcome the general physical poverty of Quebec and make available the pooled wealth of its great but scattered riches, its minerals and its water power.

Throughout the decade no one, not the most percipient, knew what the outcome of *nationalisme* and *séparatisme* would be.[6] In 1966 Premier Jean Lesage, leader of the Quiet Revolution, was defeated by the older *nationalisme* of the Union Nationale because he had reformed too much. Yet the older *nationalisme* proved too conservative. The *séparatiste* Parti Québecois emerged in the election of 1970 with 24 per cent of the popular vote. Then in October of that year cells of the Front de Libération du Québec, a terrorist organization which, following the line of action of terrorists, had perpetrated sporadic bombings since 1963, kidnapped James Cross of the British diplomatic service, and kidnapped and murdered Pierre Laporte of the Quebec cabinet. Charles de Gaulle's calculated discourtesy in his cry of "Vive le Québec libre," while the guest of Canada in 1967, had opened some eyes. But for most Canadians it took the bomb flashes in Montreal and the rosary chain that garotted Pierre Laporte to reveal the realities of the poverty of Quebec and the passions of *nationalisme.*

6. The author foresaw and opposed the secession of Quebec in 1964; his paper was printed in the *Queen's Quarterly,* Winter 1965, under the title, "The Conservative Principle in Confederation." He was soundly taken to task for his bluntness: *Canadian Annual Review,* 1964, p. 92.

III

The perception of reality is, however, the beginning of hope. But there were other realities than the friction exerted by French Canada on the development of Canadian destiny that affected the momentum of Canadian nationality. One was the decline, the near-extinction, of British influence in Canada. This was not merely a matter of sentiment, although it was that also for many Canadians and not just those of British descent. It was, in fact, objective. The character of modern Britain awaits historical definition, even more than does that of modern France and Europe, all three the matrix of the legal and political heritage of modern Canada. Something, however, of what Canada owed to Britain might be stated for the decade past. One debt, of course, was the constitution of Canadian government, as that functioned in the central and the provincial governments, under, it is true, increasing criticism. Another, becoming more important in retrospect, was the mode of British investment on which Canada flourished down to 1914. British capital left control of Canadian enterprise largely in Canadian hands, unlike the practice of American investment. A third was the concurrent decline of the Commonwealth and the monarchy in the esteem of many Canadians. What the latter meant for allegiance and citizenship in Canada will be taken up later. The fading of the Commonwealth, that long sunset of Empire, and Britain's seeking entry into the European Common Market, meant that Canada was on its own in America.

There could be, then, no doubt about the fact of the decline, not only of British influence but also of British interest in Canada. The Canadian visitor to the United Kingdom, however cordially welcomed, sensed in the British mind an indifference to Canada's fate that had a forbidding touch of finality. The British, after all, were the world's greatest realists; their scent for where power lay was unexcelled, as their turning to Europe and the Common Market signified. Did they doubt the power, the will, of Canada to survive? Perhaps they did, but they politely left it to the event to declare.

Certainly many British people quietly resented the unhelpful protests of the Diefenbaker government at the beginning of the decade against the British proposal to join the European Common Market, and some resented Canada's stand on the membership of South Africa in the Commonwealth. Few Canadians saw that ties with Europe might replace those with Britain—certainly the members of the Trudeau government did not when they diminished Canada's standing in Europe by their one-sided reduction of the Canadian forces in NATO.

The objective significance of British indifference was, however, of first importance. The British influence on Canada, from the days of Durham and of Monck, had always added to the momentum of Canadian nationality. It had not been a friction, a check on that momentum. Moreover, Canada had peculiar need for moral and diplomatic ties with the world outside North America, lest it find itself alone with the American colossus. The recognition of the People's Republic of China, so long delayed, was an example of the perception of the need at the end of the decade. But Britain had been the strongest of such ties, the brightest of Canada's windows on the world. It was a prime Canadian interest to keep the tie strong, the window clear; yet since 1961 the tie had weakened, the window darkened.

IV

To the friction of French Canadian *séparatisme* and the loss of the momentum Britain once afforded, there was to be added the friction, gravitational, inescapable, and unceasing, which the United States increasingly exerted on Canadian destiny. Nor was that friction merely a growing drag on Canadian momentum; it was at once more complex and more insidious. To a great degree it augmented the friction of French Canadian *séparatisme* and, if removed, would at least diminish that challenge to Canadian nationality. But at the same time that it reinforced the *séparatiste* challenge, it also sapped the very juice of Canadian life. The American friction was the chief brake on Canadian momentum, the greatest menace to Canadian nationality.

No subject, therefore, was more important to Canadian destiny.

The reconciliation of French Canadian nationalism with Canadian nationality might at least be postulated; how that nationality could survive the drag of what could only be called the "imperialism" of American investment was not as readily to be stated.

To attempt an explanation of the friction the United States exerted on Canadian momentum, one must first note that there was a time when the United States, like Britain, gave momentum to Canadian nationality. The very existence of the United States, independent, expansive, messianic, made it impossible, as Durham had noted and as Canadian statesmen thereafter knew, that Canada could be left in colonial torpidity. In fact, as the Fathers of Confederation, taking in the rapt eloquence of Thomas D'Arcy McGee and prompted by Lord Monck, were well aware, Canada had to become a North American nation itself, so far as possible as free and progressive as the United States.

Moreover, Canada in many literal, if often subtle, ways was an offspring of the United States. Quebec, after all, was conquered and, even more, held in the interests chiefly of the American colonies, one of the first strokes of American manifest destiny. Canada was actually, if negatively, as much a product of the War of Independence as the United States itself, because without that war there would have been no Canada as a separate political entity with a distinctive anti-revolutionary tradition. The Loyalists, Americans of Americans, were the foundation of English Canada and the creators therefore equally with the French of the quality of Canadian nationality. The colonial constitutions, in their working if not in all details, were simply the old colonial legislatures, and on the same model as the new legislatures of the states of the Union, except that governor and legislative councils were appointive, not elective. It was not surprising that Canadian reformers before 1837 thought the changes small that would give Canadian legislatures the popular vigour of the American; it would be enough simply to change the practice of appointment to that of election. What wonder that Canadians from time to time have asked themselves whether it might be well to change to the American constitutional pattern.

It would be even more revealing to go into the ties of blood, business, speech, and ideas. Suffice it to say that the general outcome of the relationship was that Canada was not only French and British, but also, and by no means less, American. That was one reason, as at least a correction to the over-emphasis on British origins in the days of imperial sentiment from the 1880's to the 1920's, that John W. Dafoe could entitle a small volume of lectures delivered in 1934, *Canada: An American Nation*.

Moreover, Canada's American strain did not act as a friction on the momentum of national destiny, and for two reasons. One was that American influence and American example did not in fact impede the independence of Canada in America. The effect was paradoxical. Rather than vitiating Canadian nationality by over-shadowing it with American numbers and forms, Canada's American heritage inoculated the Canadian body politic against American example. Canada was, to an extent, immunized by pervasive and persistent contact with American life. The second reason, as already touched on, was that the presence of the United States led Great Britain to follow the instincts of its liberal imperialists like Durham and Monck, and fit Canada as rapidly as possible for as much independence as Canada might claim, while still serving, good-naturedly and not without risk as late as the Venezuelan crisis of 1896, as a make-weight to American pressure.

After 1921 or so, however, the United States ceased to add to Canadian momentum, and became, unconsciously and in many ways slow to be perceived, the chief drag on Canadian independence.[7] There are evident reasons for this. One was a continuing difference between the two countries. In the American system private right traditionally tends to prevail over public policy; to a

7. Canadian continentalists, if any should read this commentary, may be moved to think the writer anti-American. It is not his wish to seem so; it is, however, his intent to oppose certain forms and degrees of continentalism.

great degree American government was created to safeguard private rights. In Canada public policy may and sometimes does prevail over private right; Canadian government traditionally has been charged with protecting the common welfare ("peace, order and good government"). Perhaps the best example of the difference is the considerable socialist strain in Canadian political thought, and the existence of two semi-socialist governments in Canada at the moment (Manitoba and Saskatchewan). Another was that in the United States increasingly the pursuit of simple profit has replaced the original Jeffersonian "pursuit of happiness." Canadians, particularly French Canadians, tend to think that the object of profit, or of any form of earning, is to be able to enjoy the good life as one understands it; they are, in short, prepared to be lazy. The result of the difference is an abundance of American capital and managerial skill well able to take over from less well funded and less efficient Canadians.

Moreover, the Canadian policy of nationalism combined with undefined continentalism, begun in the 1920's, was to prove a trap in the 1960's. The nationalism of William Lyon Mackenzie King and O. D. Skelton, the reciprocity of W. S. Fielding and the present-day freer trade of Professor Harry G. Johnson, the policy of good neighbourhood of George Brown and of Franklin D. Roosevelt, had led to ever-increasing American control. By 1971 some thoughtful and reasonable Canadians considered the American penetration and irradiation of Canadian life the greatest menace to the continued existence of Canada as an independent nation, greater even than Quebec *séparatisme*.

Why and how, then, had the United States become a major friction in Canadian destiny? That process may really have begun in 1887, when American manifest destiny, up to that time if anything a stimulant to the growth of Canadian nationality, lost that robust name of aggressive nationalist menace and became rather the insidious threat called "continentalism." Manifest destiny was geo-political, military, messianic: Jefferson dispatching Lewis and

Clark to the Pacific, American squatters on San Juan Island. That could, until the Boer War tied Great Britain's hands, be countered in its own terms with more or less success. (The less the success, the greater the stimulus to Canadian national feeling, as contemporary Canadian reaction to the various boundary awards showed.) Continentalism, however, was geographical and economic, a matter of certain people making profits, or certain Canadians having profitable relations with American capital. Its character is evident from its dual paternity. One parent was Goldwin Smith, a renegade Englishman of trenchant mind and nervous prose style, who perversely chose to live in Canada in the sure faith that it must become part of the United States. The other was Samuel J. Ritchie, a New York businessman interested in the great ore body found at Sudbury, Ontario, in 1883. Smith, trapped in the firm dogmas of classical Liberalism, never took the trouble to learn the importance of east-west ties in Canada; Ritchie was one of the first of those American entrepreneurs interested in developing Canadian natural resources for American use.[8]

The early flare-up of continentalism, with its political offspring, commercial union, was defeated in the Canadian general election of 1891, and even reciprocity was finally repudiated, as it seemed, in the general election of 1911. Economic continentalism was to persist, however, in the growth of the forest and mineral industries fostered by American capital invited to create employment in Canada, and in manufacturing plants set up within the Canadian tariff. Heretofore most of Canadian industry had been developed not in this way but by native enterprise and Canadian or British capital. But after the decline of British investment following the First World War and the nationalization of the Canadian Northern and Grand Trunk railways, with the consequent blow to Canadian

8. Goldwin Smith's *Canada and the Canadian Question* (Toronto, 1891), however, remains the most trenchant analysis of Canada since Confederation. For Ritchie, see O. D. Skelton, *Life and Letters of Sir Wilfrid Laurier* (London, 1922), pp. 370–71; also Morris Zaslow, *The Opening of the Canadian North, 1870-1914* (Toronto, 1971), pp. 155 and 158.

credit in London, American investment so grew in scope and size as to take on a veritable continentalist aspect. It became increasingly the source of credit underpinning both governments and industry in Canada and after the reciprocity agreement of 1936 still more so, dramatically so, in the two decades before 1971. Until the last decade the hidden fallacy of continentalism, that it is simply a beneficent form of free trade, had not been revealed in its first manifestations; it remained for the decade of the 1960's to reveal it for what it was: the classic use of free trade to subordinate a weaker economy to a stronger, to "colonize" it.

After 1961, from this ever-growing dependence on American investment, accompanied more and more by direction of the Canadian economy by Americans and the steady vitiation of Canadian national life by American technology and its inevitable running dog, American advertising, there began a crescendo of apprehension about the fate of Canada. The alarm was first sounded by James E. Coyne, governor of the Bank of Canada; it was re-echoed time after time by Walter Gordon, architect of the return of the Liberal party to office in 1963, and a member of the Liberal cabinet until 1967. It was Gordon (with the assistance of the economist Melville Watkins) who, especially in his *A Choice for Canada* (1966), began the process of analysing and exposing the extraordinary degree to which American capital had permeated and come to dominate Canadian economic life. The forebodings of imminent doom found expression in accents of the gravest pessimism in George Grant's *A Lament for a Nation* (1965) and in the Gibbonian prose, polished and plangent, of Donald Creighton's *Canada's First Hundred Years* (1970). (If the Canadian nation was indeed to disappear, its demise had at least been celebrated in the grand manner.)

So strong a sense of apprehension, so strongly expressed by leading public men, by a philosopher and by an historian, and constantly discussed in press, radio, and television, would surely signal the end of a society less immune to its own neuroses than the

Canadian. Fortunate in this respect at least, Canadians had never taken Canada for granted, or ever accepted it as final. Canada was from its depths experimental and conditional. (Yet it moved; the momentum carried.)

Accordingly, towards the last three years of the decade two results began to take shape. One was a growing manifestation of Canadian nationality, a spreading concern to save Canada for Canadians. Because of the prominence of Melville Watkins and the "Waffle" group in the New Democratic Party, it was said by some continentalist Canadians that this outburst of Canadian nationalism was monopolized by the Left. In fact, the feeling was evident in all parties and all aspects of Canadian society; it did not merely represent a Socialist wish to "nationalize." It was a widespread response to a realization that unrestrained continentalism meant the end of Canadian nationality. It was in essence an attempt to re-state and re-affirm the national aspirations, long held but clearly now inadequate, in terms that would take account at once of the French fact in Canadian life, the unintended and unwanted overwhelming of Canada by American control of Canadian economy, and the Gadarene rush of technology, pollution, and poverty that was suddenly seen as the concomitant of affluence. The other result was a considered and calculated estimate and rejection of continentalism—by many, of continentalism in all its aspects, including the unbridled growth, or appetite, of the American economic culture. Investment was a good thing, and Canada fortunate to be able to call on it, but in fact it had come to mean foreign control, direction by multinational corporations which seemed able to evade all political control, and which used Canadian resources and Canadian earnings for their own purposes. The reasons for the rejection were varied and mixed: simple national sentiment, socialist policies, an anti-American feeling sprung from opposition to the Vietnam war and from a feeling that the United States had become an armed imperialism pressing on friends and rivals alike.

V

Of these reasons, the chief was a rather unexpected recovery of a sense of Canadian nationality, or perhaps the gaining of a new grasp of the momentum of national life. For the great majority for whom that was the heart of the matter, nationality did not descend into nationalism. Canadians, because of their situation in the world, had special reasons to be internationalist in outlook, and to distrust nationalism at home or abroad.

The fervour of pure nationalism, linguistic, racial, or chauvinistic, could have no other result in Canada but, at the least, the separation of French and English.[9] Nor did the revival of a sense of nationality necessarily entail anti-Americanism, in the sense of hostility to the American government or to Americans in general; the symbiosis of Canada and the United States was recognized to admit at once of independence and interdependence. What nationalism called for was a re-assessment and re-formulation of the Canadian experiment, exemplified in the imaginative exploration of man's condition in Expo and in the attempts throughout the decade to amend the federal constitution in the new terms of Canadian politics and life, from Premier John Robarts' Confederation of Tomorrow Conference in 1967 to the inquiry, still going on in 1971, into ways of amending the constitution.[10]

This process of re-assessment and revision was only in its beginning, but certain re-assertions and re-statements could already be noted. The election in 1968 of Pierre Elliott Trudeau on a platform peculiarly personal was a demand for re-assertion of the Canadian federal union in such new terms as might be found necessary. The passage of the Official Languages Act the next year was one expression of a new character for the federal union; it was henceforth to be not only the political union of ten provinces, but also a cultural union of two language groups, each having all the aspects of

9. It was presumably, in part at least, because of this that Pierre Elliott Trudeau, with his experience of French *nationalisme*, was so carefully and so frigidly anti-nationalistic.

10. The attempt still went on at the time of writing, a sure indication that the ferment of Canadian life had not yet crystallized.

a nation but finding its respective political independence in federal union. Both changes were made out of the experience of the past century's history of Anglo-French relations in Canada. Yet they already seemed small in face of the need, if the federal union were to prove capable of preserving itself, of dealing with the unrest and poverty of much of French Quebec.

By the end of the decade, however, no step to deal with continentalism, Canadian and American, matched Prime Minister Trudeau's rigid federalism or the formal adoption of bilingualism. Indeed, the question must be raised whether Canada had demonstrated the will to survive an easy and largely unintended takeover by its gigantic, much pre-occupied neigbour. One example will suffice. Two American publications with Canadian editions, *Time* and *Reader's Digest,* protested the "proposed" imposition, in 1962, of a tax on Canadian advertising in foreign magazines, an attempt to give Canadian periodicals some relief from the competition of American magazines. The Canadian government capitulated under the pressure in 1965, and exempted the Canadian editions of the two publications from the tax. Why was it done? In the first place, the government of the day was Liberal, always disposed to continentalism, and devoted to the policy of "quiet diplomacy," which might be quiet through being submissive. In the second place, it on this occasion feared for the success of the negotiation for the Automotive Agreement, which established free exchange of parts between American and Canadian auto plants. Further, the two publishers could threaten to buy the glossy paper for the Canadian runs from American rather than Canadian manufacturers. Moreover, Canadians were addicted readers by long habit of both American periodicals. Thus Canadian periodicals, necessary for the refinement of Canadian public opinion, were sacrificed, not without reason, but without sufficient reason.

It was such action of men in high places, together with the failure of Canadians to protest, that justified the pessimism, not to say fatalism, of Grant and Creighton. Yet such exercises in continentalism helped provoke the resurgence of national feeling and an analysis of continentalism for what it was, a betrayal of Canadian destiny and identity.

That analysis, so far as it had proceeded, was roughly as follows. In an economic world devoted to the equation of prosperity with growth, the Canadian economy was dependent on investment, and by habit especially on foreign investment. Canadian investors preferred certain of the securer forms of investment, whether Canadian or foreign. In general, they did not speculate on "risk" investments. Thus, although very good savers, they financed the Canadian economy only in part, if perhaps capable of doing so from their own resources. The great source of foreign investment, and until recently almost the only one, since the decline of British investment, was the United States. Moreover, American investors were largely concerned to invest in resource industries, partly to provide raw materials for American consumers of such materials. As a result, investment in Canada, chiefly in the primary industries, wood pulp, mining, and particularly oil, had been almost wholly American. The proportion of American investment in such Canadian industries and even in manufacturing was, from the point of view of Canadian nationality, deeply disturbing.[11]

11. The amount of investment was disturbing for two reasons, one practical, one moral. The practical one, stressed by Walter Gordon, was that the payment of interest and dividends might exceed, indeed promised to do so, what Canada could pay in foreign exchange in a given year. The moral, stressed here, is that the involvement of Canadian businessmen and politicians with foreign investors might be so great, if not already so, as to destroy the national will for independence.

The best analysis of the situation known to the writer is that by Kari Levitt, *Silent Surrender* (Toronto, 1970). Although her conclusion is that Canada has been, and is being, economically "colonized" by American capital, with which the writer agrees, Dr. Levitt was not concerned to deal with the purchase by Americans of water-front property, and too early to note the ultimate take-over—the invasion of the western provinces by Texan undertakers buying up profitable funeral parlours.

Dr. Levitt states (pp. 61–62) that some 60 per cent of Canada's manufacturing industry, 70 per cent of its petroleum and natural gas industry, and 60 per cent of its mining and smelting industry are "now" controlled by foreign corporations.

It was deeply disturbing because political independence in the last resort rested on a reasonable degree of economic autonomy. The matter, however, called for careful analysis. In the first place, in the economy of today—perhaps itself something to be discarded or at least modified—investment was to be welcomed. Second, insofar as investment was simply money risked in a particular enterprise, it did not matter whether the source was foreign or domestic, except, on occasion, in terms of foreign exchange. Money was money; investment was investment. From this point of view Canada was fortunate to have attracted so much American investment, as it was fortunate in the last century to have had British investment. True, it would no doubt have been better—that is, cosier–to have developed only by Canadian savings and investment, but in default of that, American investment had served the purpose very well. So would German, Japanese, or Tibetan investment.

The rub was, however, that American investment had been very different in method from British. The British had lent money to earn interest and regain the principal, which on the whole they did until the débâcle of the Grand Trunk and Grand Trunk Pacific railways. The American had proved no such investor. He did not, as a rule and except in government borrowings, lend in the form of bonds. He invested directly and held his investment in equity stock. Thus American investment was followed by perpetual American ownership and by American control. American-owned industries, situated and operating in Canada, sometimes dominating, often creating, Canadian towns, were not Canadian except in law and by residence, even when the managers of such industries conducted their affairs as "good corporate citizens." This circumstance in itself was a diminution of Canada and of the Canadians who served in these industries. Tolerable up to a certain point in any society, American control in the decade of the 1960's had passed the point of tolerance and had become an urgent, if unintended, danger to Canadian national life.

Nor did the matter end with control. American control was confirmed by American management. Bland, likeable American top staff, carefully schooled, like British imperial civil servants in the nineteenth century, to take charge anywhere in the world, dominated not only the industries but also the communities in the wood pulp, oil, or mining towns. Canadians, if trained in management by such American experts, were prepared, not necessarily for Canadian appointments, but to be sent wherever the parent corporations needed them—Brazil, Indonesia, Europe, even the United States. They had no doubt become efficient managerial staff, but they tended to become denationalized, while the Americans remained American, rarely taking on the colour of the environment, rarely forgetting the national source from which they came.

There was to be said in defence of American investment (and it was often said, particularly by Canadian politicians), that it created employment for Canadians beyond what could have been done by Canadian capital alone. This was true, but it was not the whole truth. Foreign capital gave employment, to be sure; it also both denied employment to some and, as Eric Kierans pointed out on resigning from the federal cabinet over this issue in 1971, American investment tended to be in forms which were capital-intensive, not labour-intensive. The employment created was largely for unskilled or semi-skilled workers; much investment, indeed, created little employment.[12] But the retention of control of management by Americans led to complaints of the employment of Americans of other expertise, as in the building of the iron-ore railway from Sept Iles to Schefferville, or in oil exploration, thus denying employment to Canadians of the higher skills and professions. The tendency of American investment was thus to stunt Canadian entrepreneurial, managerial, and professional so-

12. The denial of employment of course comes through the use of American staff of managerial and technological skill and experience, as in the oil industry, in itself often both desirable and necessary in the beginning. The failure to employ less skilled workers arises from the preponderance of American investment in resource rather than manufacturing industries. In primary industries the need for labour tends to be less than in secondary.

ciety, and make Canadians, like the people of other countries, the proletariat of American capital. This tendency was, of course, most evident in Quebec, where English Canadians combined with Americans as controlling elements in finance and industry.

Nor did the effects of American control of Canadian industries end there. The American government, normally concerned to preserve the image of the United States as the friend of free countries and free enterprise, had repeatedly treated American companies in Canada—as elsewhere—simply as parts of American firms operating in the United States under American law. In export policy they followed American, not Canadian, law; they sometimes submitted to American anti-trust laws; they allowed the American government to use their Canadian savings as American funds. This exercise of extra-territorial power was at once a measure of that American imperialism which since the Second World War had made Americans disliked, whatever benefits their capital conferred in Canada or in Europe; more to the point, it was also the measure of the subservience to which unguarded continentalism had brought Canada. Neither Mexico nor British Guiana, for example, had been willing to endure such treatment from Americans or from Canadians.[13]

Such a friction as that created by American control of a major part of Canadian economic life clearly threatened to bring the momentum of Canadian nationality to an early stop; some observers said in five years, some in ten. What, then, was to be said of a situation so serious, so nearly desperate?

VI

The first matter to be dealt with was the charge of anti-Americanism instantly levelled by Canadian continentalists at anyone who ventured to speak firmly on American-Canadian relations. This charge could in the first place be dealt with briefly, and in American terms. If to be a Canadian nationalist was to be opposed

13. The references are to the Mexican take-over of American oil companies, and Guianan take-over of the Aluminum Company of Canada.

to American control of the Canadian economy, then Canadian continentalists might make the most of it. In the second place, to be Canadian was not to scorn, or even dislike, American culture, nor was it to be anti-American in the sense of being hostile to the United States or to Americans as persons. It was simply to be Canadian; and Americans, themselves among the most nationalistic of people, would understand that very well, even if Canadian continentalists did not. Hostility between two countries so interdependent would not only be harmful, not least to Canada; it would also be degrading for both peoples as civilized communities. It was so out of discussion that it was irrelevant and had nothing to do with American-Canadian relations.

There were in fact only two issues of magnitude. One was that known as continentalism. That, to be dealt with, had to be cut up into its various aspects. The primary aspect of continentalism was defence. On this point a Canadian nationalist might well be a continentalist. To hold that Canada could not in its own interest, and ought not as an American nation, imperil the security of the United States was a defensible view. To act on that belief was to consider Canada's own security; hence NATO and NORAD were both Canadian interests and might well be maintained,[14] both as a national interest and as an obligation to a neighbour.

In all other respects, however, continentalism as a policy, if not as a habit of daily life, was a continuing menace to Canadian nationality. It had been so since at least 1887, and might be so indefinitely. Canadian nationality therefore required that it always be resisted, and accepted if at all only for particular occasions and on limited terms. Anything like commercial union, the Automotive Agreement, the proposed "continental energy pact," was, or would be, a surrender of Canadian sovereignty, and contrary to national policy. The natural resources of Canada were not "continental"; they were Canadian. They were continental only in the sense that

14. This view is in conflict with that held by certain Canadian thinkers, notably Professor James Eayrs, and to some degree with that of the present government of Canada since 1969.

Canada was part of the North American continent. If for sale, they were for sale to any buyer in the world.

The second matter was that of the techniques of American investment and American control of that investment abroad, techniques eagerly followed in the last years of the decade by Japanese investors in Canada. Those methods were by 1970 well known in Canada, and were in simple terms, equity rather than debt investment, and the prevalence, in most cases, of American management of American firms operating under Canadian law in Canada with Canadian labour. Equity investment remained American; it was not purchasable or repayable by Canadians, as were bonds; it was therefore perpetually under American control. American management was justified by its high skill, but skills could be learned, as they were in companies that were "good corporate citizens."

In all this there was little reason to be hostile to American, or other foreign investment. It was the duty of the businessman to make the best deals he could. If the deals were bad deals for Canada, the fault lay with the Canadians who had accepted them. Canadian businessmen and Canadian politicians had invited Americans to invest in Canada and had allowed them to do so on their own terms. The one major exception were those enterprises held to be "strategic," such as banking, insurance, the daily press —not, oddly enough, publishing, which at the end of the decade began to go the way of oil and wood pulp.[15] It was notorious by

15. What provoked the agitation with respect to publishing was the sale of Ryerson Press, owned by the United Church of Canada, to an American buyer, and the announcement of Mr. J. G. McClelland, of McClelland & Stewart, Ltd., publishers, that he could not obtain from Canadian banks the funds necessary to continue the operation of his historic family firm. The result was the appointment of a Royal Commission of Enquiry by the government of Ontario. It quickly recommended, before making its report, that a low interest loan be made by the government to the firm. This was promptly done, and Canadian control maintained. The implications of this action were, of course, wide-ranging. But even more pertinent to the theme of this commentary was the Commission's discovery that American ownership of agencies to distribute books and periodicals led not only to American control, but the almost exclusive distribution of American material.

the end of the 1960's that Canada exercised perhaps less control over foreign investment than any other developed country in the world. The only discernible explanation for the behaviour on the part of Canadian businessmen and politicians that had led to such a situation was that employment had to be provided in the backward parts of the country and that the provinces which controlled natural resources were competing for American investment. (It is apparent that the eagerness of the provinces of the depressed regions of Canada for investment for development and employment, especially if aggravated, as it has been, by the lack of Canadian funds from the over-conservative and over-centralized Canadian banks, made the control and limitation of foreign control exceedingly difficult.) With the exception of the undoubted need for employment, all other reasons for the degree of foreign ownership and control were in fact grounds for a most formidable indictment of Canadian businessmen and politicians.

Reference to foreign purchase of Canadian publishing firms raises the question of the actual desirability of foreign investment. Against the two most recently purchased Canadian firms there might in one case be alleged some inefficiency, in the other simply the choice of the more attractive offer. In terms of business, everything was open and above board, and nothing is to be said. But will foreign ownership and control affect the future of Canadian writing adversely, or beneficially? There will be more capital available, and no doubt better management. But will there be any consideration of anything but profit, of Canadian taste, interests, and aspirations? Possibly not: it is the same thing, put more concisely and vividly, as with all foreign control.

Related is the recently much publicized employment of foreign scholars in Canadian universities. In certain departments of certain universities, in considerable numbers, this has resulted in foreign control, and, it is alleged, further employment of foreign scholars from foreign universities known to the foreign heads of departments (no doubt for perfectly understandable reasons). What is to be said? Canadian universities needed these people, and were fortunate to be able to attract them; any general indictment of them and their services would be uncivilized. Knowledge is in general international, and any university benefits from some mixture of scholars of different backgrounds. The question is purely a practical one, one of control, of position, of personality, even of certain subjects. Political science, for example—although the study of Canadian literature is an equally sore point—was quite different from the same subject in the United States, and for good reason, as the political traditions and systems of the two countries are quite different. It was, however, a relatively undeveloped subject in Canada, yet a newly popular one. It was accordingly one in which foreign scholars were particularly in demand, and one in which foreign control is most evident. The result could be the introduction of an alien tradition into Canadian university teaching. Again, the parallel with business is evident. Canada had not developed its own resources, and suddenly had to make good the deficiency by an excessive employment of scholars from abroad. In general, the result was a strengthening of Canadian universities; in particular cases, it may lead to a break with Canadian traditions, and foreign control of an important area of Canadian thought. As in investment, the fault is largely Canadian; the result, foreign control.

With such examples, the indictment of those who controlled business and government in Canada was complete by 1971. If foreign investment was desirable, the ballooning degree of foreign ownership and control was not. The difficulty lay not so much in devising means to regulate foreign investment and control, but in ensuring that Canadian businessmen and politicians would make adequate regulations, or abide by them if made. What foreign control existed could be contained, and safeguards against future foreign control might readily be constructed from foreign example. The necessary measures to deal with the situation at the end of the decade could have been stated as if in a textbook: (1) that all companies operating in Canada be required to have 51 per cent of their boards of directors citizens of Canada (51 per cent is cited as that commonly used; 75 per cent at least is necessary to ensure control); (2) that no foreigner should be allowed to own equity stock in a company operating under Canadian law; (3) that if any company operating under Canadian law were to decline to sell its products anywhere because of the requirements of the law of another state than Canada, or were to surrender to another government retained savings earned in Canada, it should become, at the market value of its stock at the time of such action, the property of the Canadian Development Corporation, when established; (4) that if foreign-owned and foreign-controlled companies operating in Canada at the time of the changes proposed above failed to conform with such laws within a stated time, say ten to fifteen years, they should become the property of the Canadian Development Corporation at a fair market value to be set by a Canadian board of arbitration.

Complementary to, and following from this, it would have been necessary to require that, over a reasonable period, all trade unions in Canada end their administrative and financial ties with foreign unions. Further, to terminate foreign control and ensure that foreign investment would give the greatest possible employment to Canadians, no foreign expert or professional should be employed by any company operating under Canadian law except on licence from the Canadian government. To the same end, such companies should be required to conduct research necessary to their operations in Canada or to pay a special tax for the support of government research in Canada. Finally, no foreign purchase of Canadian industry, land, or other resource, should be permitted except on licence from the appropriate government.

Such measures would be simple and enforceable; they would neither be unfair to foreign investors nor discourage foreign investment unduly. Nor would they be out of line with what such countries as Sweden, France, and Japan already required of foreign investors.[16] Only in Canada would they seem drastic.

16. The scholarly examination of the economic position of foreign ownership in Canada up to the mid-sixties is that by A. E. Safarian, *Foreign Owner-*

Clearly, the last remarks pointed to an unusual situation in Canada. Why should a country with a history so distinctive, a position so happy, a natural endowment so great, be so ready a victim of a foreign take-over unparalleled in extent and degree? The question both lacked and required extensive investigation, but answers might be divined with some assurance. One was that the situation was not created by Americans. It was the doing of Canadians, Canadian businessmen and Canadian politicians, the latter more often than not provincial, seeking local industries to ensure votes. They were aided and abetted by the Canadian public, which until recently had not protested their performance, but rather applauded it. The political party, for example, which has been most prone to continentalism, the Liberal party, has been in power by the will of the Canadian electorate fifty-four out of the seventy-four years since 1896.

The second was that Canadian businessmen and Canadian politicians had become accustomed to practise what to a Canadian nationalist might seem a casual semi-treason in their operations with foreign capital and foreign-controlled firms. Businessmen (bankers and brokers especially) had become accustomed to find profit in borrowing from and selling to the United States. Business

---

ship of Canadian Industry (Toronto, 1966). Good studies of the problem and the control of foreign ownership are Peter Russell, ed., *Nationalism in Canada* (Toronto 1966); W. L. Gordon, *A Choice for Canada* (Toronto, 1966); Melville Watkins *et al.*, *Foreign Ownership and the Structure of Canadian Industry* (Ottawa, 1968), Section III, chap. 2; Safarian, "Foreign Investment in Canada: Some Myths," *Journal of Canadian Studies*, August, 1971.

As this essay went to press the *Canadian Forum*, November 12, 1971, published what seemed to be a draft in part of the study of the control of foreign ownership ordered by Hon. Herbert Gray of the Canadian government. It is a comprehensive and sophisticated study of the whole matter, and recommends a "screening" agency to supervise the increase and the domestic growth of foreign owned and controlled firms. At the moment of writing its adoption or rejection by the Cabinet had not been formally announced. Its proposal of a screening agency, however, had been questioned and even denounced by certain provincial Premiers. Here it is only noted that the efficacy of even a "screening body" would depend upon the will with which it was used.

firms acting under national law, and sometimes asking favours of government and receiving some, might have been expected on occasion to act in the national interest. But Canadian businessmen were not often nationalists, as was made clear late in 1970 by the action of the Bank of Montreal, the bank most entwined with Canadian history, in giving its advertising account to an American firm, on the business grounds of cost and efficiency.

The situation of the politicians was more arresting. It had become increasingly evident, as historical research developed, that Canadian political parties had from time to time since the 1880's got at least part of their funds from interests in the United States.[17] With the multiplication of American-owned and American-controlled corporations, including, of course, the labour unions (many of them controlled from the United States), it was possible, since the greater part of party funds came from corporate givers (Canadian and "good corporate citizens," if by no means all American-controlled corporations), that not a few members of the Canadian Parliament (or provincial legislatures) were elected with some obligation to American interests. Indeed, it was impossible to be certain that members of Parliament in 1970 could vote on a matter affecting the special interests of foreign companies except in the manner it was supposed they would approve.[18] On the mere face of the facts of foreign ownership and the presumptive source of party funds, it was possible to doubt how independent the Parliament and government of Canada were, and how sovereign the Canadian nation. Canadian politicians, both federal and provincial, were in a situation (of which no evidence was available, in as

17. Evidence is almost impossible to find in this field, by its nature confidential and secretive. But see Waite, *Arduous Destiny: Canada, 1874–1896* (Toronto, 1970), pp. 191 and 223.

18. It would be a pleasant bit of rhetoric to recall how the legislature of Montana was once owned, so it was alleged, individually and corporately by the Anaconda Copper Company, controlled by British interests. It was equally intriguing to hear it said—the only fact here stated is that the observation, presumably untrue, was heard—that the present Prime Minister of Canada was financially aided in his campaign for the leadership of the Liberal party by an American-owned and controlled oil company.

much as politicians in Canada are not required to reveal the sources of their funds) in which the suspicion was possible, because of the extent of foreign ownership and control, that they were dependent on foreign corporations for some part of their election expenses. Only the legal requirement to declare the sources of funds would clarify a set of circumstances embarrassing to all parties, and even dangerous to the national interest.

Clearly, any danger, however slight, of political subservience in the governments and legislatures of the nation had to be averted, if Canada were to survive the American economic take-over some Canadians feared. Again, as in the matter of foreign control of the economy, the remedy might be put in terms as simple as those of a textbook. Political parties, as well as politicians, would have to be required to declare all the sources of their funds, personal and party. It would have to be made a most serious offence for any politician or party to accept funds from a foreign source, or a foreign-controlled Canadian corporation, and for such sources to furnish them. Prosecution for failure to report, and for the use of funds from, or the giving of funds by, foreign persons or foreign-controlled corporations or unions, would be made the responsibility of the Chief Electoral Officer. If the result was, as it would be, the drying-up of corporate contributions, then public funds should be provided for electoral expenses. Such measures might seem drastic by the weak standards of the past. But those standards, along with continentalism, had produced such conditions that only harsh measures could offer any hope of cure. The fibre of Canadian life had been slackened, the national will enervated, the momentum of Canadian destiny slowed until it was apparent that Canada could easily become, like other states on the two continents, a mere outpost of American business and policy.

VII

Such was the extent of the American friction on Canadian momentum in 1971. What, then, remained of the Canada that had existed, or had been thought to exist, in 1961? Much, it could be claimed. First was the fortuitous but happy fact that no one, certainly not the United States, wished to deprive Canada of its national existence, or Canadian society of its own peculiar character. The matter was one of Canadian will to survive, at the end of a decade in which the national will and nerve of Canada had seemed at their lowest point, despite Expo, despite October 18, 1970, and the rally of the nation to the proclamation of the War Measures Act. Second, the elements that seemed permanent in 1961 were still as present, and perhaps as influential, in 1971.

The first of those elements in importance was the northern environment, the geographic conditions of Canadian life. These largely determined the economic lives of English and French Canadians alike, and only political independence promised that either could use Canadian resources for Canadian purposes. But the unifying effects of environment had been challenged, squarely and dramatically, by French *séparatisme*, or *indépendantisme*. *Séparatisme*, at its most fundamental, was, there was some reason to think, the assertion of Quebec's determination to be part of Canada in full and equal participation in Canadian life, but on French terms. Even if Quebec should separate, it would probably be in terms of association which could lead to a new integration in a new partnership to develop the northern half of the continent in ways suitable for a national existence and not just as a region subordinate to the American market. The common need of French and English Canada was to resist American control, because independence of the United States was the *sine qua non* of the existence of either; indeed, the weakness shown by English Canada in being unable to resist American control without the British counterweight had strengthened, if not created, French *séparatisme*. If Canada as a whole were to bring American ownership and control under appropriate regulation, *séparatisme* would be weakened and there would be a beginning to the creation of that realistic and sophisticated understanding and co-operation between French and English without which Canada could at best only partly exist.

The results of urbanization raised a question more difficult to answer, but it was noteworthy that Canada, in becoming urban, was in a real sense returning to its origins. Canada was in the beginning a country of trading posts, fishing stations, and lumber ports handling the primary commerce of the continent. Farming was at first and for long subordinate to the great staples. As the essential nature of the city is concentration for exchange and communication, and as no city can exist without a hinterland, Canada in reverting to city life and vast hinterlands was, if in a new phase of urban life, returning to its original nature. The century of agricultural predominance was, it would seem, a deviation from its fundamental history. Urbanization restored an original character, and the development of the North not only re-affirmed the importance of that region in Canadian history and character, but gave the great new cities wider hinterlands by which to live.

The next feature in importance was the concept of a nationality made up as a mosaic of peoples and a plurality of cultures. It was an unusual concept, which flew in the face of most human experience and had in fact cost Canada much. Yet it had continued and clarified itself, and the decade's agonies had been part of that process. Clarification called for insight and redefinition, and these were possible in Canada, because the mosaic principle had won ever wider acceptance among Canadians, not just as a rationalization of a failure to assimilate, but as an expression of the actual experience of the people making up Canada. Basic to Canadian life was the duality of English and French and the indefinite perpetuation of the cultures of other groups. In this fact, not in a failure of assimilation, was the root of the mosaic principle. Because it was so integral a part of Canadian life, obviously Canada stood or fell with the success or failure of the mosaic.[19]

In yet another manner was the principle of the mosaic of peoples

19. The writer is aware of the Hartzian implications of what he says. His assumptions are (1) that the "pieces" of the mosaic have a political and social context, and (2) that they must and will in time "run" in a delayed assimilation, an assimilation, however, of each to all, not to a pre-determined standard, say, British.

part of the political and social cohesion of Canadian society. That was the tradition of allegiance of British subjects to the monarch. In allegiance, national origin was of no legal importance, and ought not to have been of any practical significance, although the fact that the mosaic was "vertical" as well as horizontal revealed that it was. Canadian society and sentiment were, however, very "republican" in their preference for simplicity and equality, and to many Canadians the very terms "allegiance" and "subject" were distasteful. That essential republicanism, together with the decline of Britain and the Commonwealth, accounted for the changing significance of the monarchy in Canada. In that change, however, the inner meaning of allegiance had not been lost. It had been translated, rather, into a term more congenial to the Canadian temperament, that of citizenship. Canadian citizenship was in every way like allegiance, common, universal, never a matter of either provincial residence or national origin. All Canadians were equally Canadian citizens, whether of English, French, or any other origin.

The fusion of allegiance and citizenship took place with extreme simplicity. The tradition of monarchy had simply flowed into the sea of Canadian democracy, into "the instinctive populism of the Canadian people."[20] Beneath the late rejection of all things British, the continuing and "colonial" deference to most things American, there lay in Canadians an ultimate independence, a resolution, exploding fiercely from time to time, that government and society should conform to their own plain taste in tone and temper. To that taste the pomp and ceremony of Edwardian, or even Georgian, England had little to offer; nor had Kennedyan pomp and circumstance much. What Canadians had not realized was that their own peculiar populism, their own conviction that government should be simple and decent, could only with difficulty find expression in the pressures and the ferocity of republican politics, with its dread theme of assassination, the accompaniment of personal power. They did not realize that political simplicity

20. I owe the phrase to a colleague from overseas.

could be expressed in the plain humanity of a Canadian monarchy, such as that exhibited by the Queen of Canada in the Northwest and Manitoba in the summer of 1970.[21]

From these things, and much else, came the Canadian momentum. What had been true in 1961 remained true in 1971. Canada possessed a unique destiny of its own. It would realize that destiny in fact if it realized it in its own consciousness, in its own will. No one else stood in the way, certainly not Americans. In days of American failure abroad and at home, there was little reason for Canadians, whatever their own faults, to be impressed by a sick republic, weary under the too vast orb of its fate. Fortunate it was then for them that they might still shelter in its lee. But once they had paid a due and proper fee by making a reasonable contribution of their own to that protection, they would be free to be themselves.

It followed, therefore, that Canadians had only to assert once more the momentum of their destiny, and the frictions which had seemed so great in the past decade, French *séparatisme* and American control, would be seen for what they really were, the French despairing of the Canadian momentum, Americans filling a vacuum left by Canadian inertia. The momentum would once more gather way. For the fact in general was that the two great frictions, French and American, were closely related and in large part a function of the third point of the historic Canadian triangle, English Canada. It had always been so. For example, Charles Buller had written confidentially of the French of Canada in his day: "the French Canadians are the natural instrument by which the Government could keep in check the democratic and American tendencies of Upper Canada."[22] Times have changed but not the historic triangle, not the dynamic tensions from which spring the

21. A fine expression of a Canadian view of the monarchy is Frank MacKinnon's "The Value of the Monarchy," *Dalhousie Review*, Summer, 1969; see also Robert Speaight, *Vanier: Soldier, Diplomat and Governor General* (Toronto, 1970), p. 431, for the Queen's comments on monarchy and democracy at Quebec in 1964.

22. Jacques Monet, *The Last Cannon Shot* (Toronto, 1970), p. 90; see also the "Conclusion," pp. 398–99.

momentum and the frictions of Canadian life. Both French and English Canada are being "colonized," the former by Anglo-American capital, the latter by American. French Canada resists; will English Canada? At the end of the sixties the question was, then, would and could English Canada–and the majority of French Canada–so act, firmly and reasonably, to ensure that foreign investment did not lead to foreign control? If they did, it would strengthen French faith in the future of Canada and thereby diminish the force of French *séparatisme*.

Canadians, English and French, had in order each to survive to reforge their unity by repeating once again the historic Canadian rejection of external control, imperial and continental, and at this time by putting further limits on a continentalism, proper and natural within limits, but which bade all too easily to become unlimited. If the frictions of the past decade continued and combined, they might well destroy Canada; if they were isolated one from another by English Canada realizing the peril and asserting itself, reasonably and firmly, the historic momentum of Canada would resume its course.[23]

23. The above essay was being prepared for the press when President Richard Nixon announced the far-reaching changes in the economic policy of the United States designed to correct the deficit in its balance of payments, in part caused by Canadian exports to that country. At this point it is possible only to acknowledge the responsibility of President Nixon to act in the best interests of the United States as conceived by his administration. One may, however, also note the implications of his act for Canadian continentalists, who may benefit from the spectacle of a nation pursuing its own best interests as it sees them. President Nixon's action may well merit the applause of Canadian nationalists.

Index

Abdication crisis, 1936: and succession, 54

Acadia: cession of, 9; war in, 8

Alaska boundary: award and Canadian humiliation, 67; award and election of 1911, 69; controversy concerning, 66–67; not settled, 65

Albany Congress, 1754, 15, 24–25

Alverstone, Richard Everard Webster, Viscount: and Alaska boundary award, 67

America: Canadian loss of heartland of, 23; European balance of power in, 8; mass culture of, 81, 85; peace with, 21; supremacy in, 23, 59, 68; united, 15. *See also* United States

American-Canadian relations: after Alaska boundary award, 68; course of, viii; depression of thirties did no damage to, 73; partition of continent and, 31

American Revolution: and allegiance in British America, 100

Americans: people of the covenant, 84

American settlers: in Upper Canada, 26; legal status of, 34; War of 1812 and, 28

Amherst, Sir Jeffrey: and Louisbourg, 1758, 14

Anaconda Copper Company, 144n

Anglican establishment: in the colonies, 34

Anglo-American empire, 15, 17–19; failure to absorb northern frontier, 95

Anglo-American settlers, 16, 18

Anglo-Americans: supremacy of, 9; traders, 11; victory of, 14

Anglo-Japanese Treaty: ended, 1921, 53

Anglo-Russian Treaty, 1825: and Alaska boundary, 65

Apartheid: impossible in Commonwealth, 56

151